OPPOSING VIEWPOINTS® SERIES

Video Games

Other Books of Related Interest:

Opposing Viewpoints Series

Censorship

Children and the Entertainment Industry

Copyright Infringement

Current Controversies Series

Blogs

Family Violence

Media Ethics

At Issue Series

Can Busy Teens Succeed Academically?

Should the Internet Be Free?

Violent Children

"Congress shall make no law . . . abridging the freedom of speech, or of the press."

First Amendment to the U.S. Constitution

The basic foundation of our democracy is the First Amendment guarantee of freedom of expression. The Opposing Viewpoints Series is dedicated to the concept of this basic freedom and the idea that it is more important to practice it than to enshrine it.

Video Games

Laurie Willis, Book Editor

GREENHAVEN PRESS
A part of Gale, Cengage Learning

GALE
CENGAGE Learning·

Detroit • New York • San Francisco • New Haven, Conn • Waterville, Maine • London

Christine Nasso, *Publisher*
Elizabeth Des Chenes, *Managing Editor*

© 2010 Greenhaven Press, a part of Gale, Cengage Learning.

Gale and Greenhaven Press are registered trademarks used herein under license.

For more information, contact:
Greenhaven Press
27500 Drake Rd.
Farmington Hills, MI 48331-3535
Or you can visit our Internet site at gale.cengage.com

For product information and technology assistance, contact us at

Gale Customer Support, 1-800-877-4253
For permission to use material from this text or product, submit all requests online at
www.cengage.com/permissions

Further permissions questions can be emailed to permissionrequest@cengage.com

Articles in Greenhaven Press anthologies are often edited for length to meet page requirements. In addition, original titles of these works are changed to clearly present the main thesis and to explicitly indicate the author's opinion. Every effort is made to ensure that Greenhaven Press accurately reflects the original intent of the authors. Every effort has been made to trace the owners of copyrighted material.

Cover photographs © Nick Veasey/Getty Images and Terry Vine/Blend Images/Getty Images.

LIBRARY OF CONGRESS CATALOGING-IN-PUBLICATION DATA

Video games / Laurie Willis, book editor.
    p. cm. -- (Opposing viewpoints)
    Includes bibliographical references and index.
    978-0-7377-4510-8 (hardcover)
    978-0-7377-4511-5 (pbk.)
    1. Video games. I. Willis, Laurie.
    GV1469.3.V526 2009
    794.8--dc22

                                                            2009019028

Printed in the United States of America
1 2 3 4 5 6 7 13 12 11 10 09

Contents

Chapter 3: What Is the Impact of Violence in Video Games?

Chapter 4: How Should Video Games Be Regulated?

Why Consider Opposing Viewpoints?

> *"The only way in which a human being can make some approach to knowing the whole of a subject is by hearing what can be said about it by persons of every variety of opinion and studying all modes in which it can be looked at by every character of mind. No wise man ever acquired his wisdom in any mode but this."*
>
> *John Stuart Mill*

In our media-intensive culture it is not difficult to find differing opinions. Thousands of newspapers and magazines and dozens of radio and television talk shows resound with differing points of view. The difficulty lies in deciding which opinion to agree with and which "experts" seem the most credible. The more inundated we become with differing opinions and claims, the more essential it is to hone critical reading and thinking skills to evaluate these ideas. Opposing Viewpoints books address this problem directly by presenting stimulating debates that can be used to enhance and teach these skills. The varied opinions contained in each book examine many different aspects of a single issue. While examining these conveniently edited opposing views, readers can develop critical thinking skills such as the ability to compare and contrast authors' credibility, facts, argumentation styles, use of persuasive techniques, and other stylistic tools. In short, the Opposing Viewpoints Series is an ideal way to attain the higher-level thinking and reading skills so essential in a culture of diverse and contradictory opinions.

In addition to providing a tool for critical thinking, Opposing Viewpoints books challenge readers to question their own strongly held opinions and assumptions. Most people form their opinions on the basis of upbringing, peer pressure, and personal, cultural, or professional bias. By reading carefully balanced opposing views, readers must directly confront new ideas as well as the opinions of those with whom they disagree. This is not to simplistically argue that everyone who reads opposing views will—or should—change his or her opinion. Instead, the series enhances readers' understanding of their own views by encouraging confrontation with opposing ideas. Careful examination of others' views can lead to the readers' understanding of the logical inconsistencies in their own opinions, perspective on why they hold an opinion, and the consideration of the possibility that their opinion requires further evaluation.

Evaluating Other Opinions

To ensure that this type of examination occurs, Opposing Viewpoints books present all types of opinions. Prominent spokespeople on different sides of each issue as well as well-known professionals from many disciplines challenge the reader. An additional goal of the series is to provide a forum for other, less known, or even unpopular viewpoints. The opinion of an ordinary person who has had to make the decision to cut off life support from a terminally ill relative, for example, may be just as valuable and provide just as much insight as a medical ethicist's professional opinion. The editors have two additional purposes in including these less known views. One, the editors encourage readers to respect others' opinions—even when not enhanced by professional credibility. It is only by reading or listening to and objectively evaluating others' ideas that one can determine whether they are worthy of consideration. Two, the inclusion of such viewpoints encourages the important critical thinking skill of objectively evaluating an author's credentials and bias. This evaluation will illuminate an author's reasons for taking a particular stance on an issue and will aid in readers' evaluation of the author's ideas.

It is our hope that these books will give readers a deeper understanding of the issues debated and an appreciation of the complexity of even seemingly simple issues when good and honest people disagree. This awareness is particularly important in a democratic society such as ours in which people enter into public debate to determine the common good. Those with whom one disagrees should not be regarded as enemies but rather as people whose views deserve careful examination and may shed light on one's own.

Thomas Jefferson once said that "difference of opinion leads to inquiry, and inquiry to truth." Jefferson, a broadly educated man, argued that "if a nation expects to be ignorant and free . . . it expects what never was and never will be." As individuals and as a nation, it is imperative that we consider the opinions of others and examine them with skill and discernment. The Opposing Viewpoints Series is intended to help readers achieve this goal.

David L. Bender and Bruno Leone,
Founders

Introduction

> *"Today's students—K through college—represent the first generations to grow up with this new technology. They have spent their entire lives surrounded by and using computers, videogames, digital music players, video cams, cell phones, and all the other toys and tools of the digital age. Today's average college grads have spent less than 5,000 hours of their lives reading, but over 10,000 hours playing video games (not to mention 20,000 hours watching TV). . . . It is now clear that as a result of this ubiquitous environment and the sheer volume of their interaction with it, today's students* think and process information fundamentally differently *from their predecessors."*
>
> —Marc Prensky,
> Digital Natives and
> Digital Immigrants, 2001.

The term "digital natives" has been coined to describe children, teens, and young adults who are growing up surrounded by technology—computers, video games, the Internet, cell phones, MP3 players, and myriad other electronic gadgets. Digital natives can't imagine a world without technology, which pervades everything they do.

In contrast, people born before the late twentieth century have been called "digital immigrants." They can remember a pre-digital world. Many have learned new technologies as they developed, but few achieve the comfort level that seems natural to digital natives. To a native, it seems that immigrants always have an "accent," often illustrated by the example of a person who calls a colleague on the phone to ask, "Did you get my e-mail?" This makes perfect sense to many digital immigrants, but seems absurd to digital natives.

In the early twenty-first century, society is at an unusual crossroads. Most adults responsible for the education of children—teachers, parents, and others—are digital immigrants, while the children they teach are digital natives. Children need to learn not only academics but also behaviors, morality, social norms, and life skills. Some digital immigrants have moved wholeheartedly into the digital age, contending that children are growing up very differently than previous generations and that educators need to adapt their methods, using technology to reach children "where they live." Other adults believe that traditional teaching methods should be maintained and that children should be shielded from the effects of technology as much as possible. Many adults take a position somewhere in the middle, acknowledging the influence of technology and attempting to keep children safe from negative aspects of technology while making use of what they see as the positive aspects.

Video games are popular with digital natives and represent one aspect of this controversy. Educators and parents question whether games are a hindrance to academic education or can be used as a tool to enhance education. They also disagree about the effects video games have on the moral and social education of children.

People on both sides of the issue point to specific games as examples to prove their point. Those who believe games can be a valuable educational tool might point to one such as *Oregon Trail*, which has been around since the 1970s and is now in its third version. Players take on the roles of settlers as they move across the United States, exploring new territory. Those concerned about the harm video games can cause might point to games in the *Grand Theft Auto* series or the *Halo* series. Both of these games are in the "first-person shooter" genre, in which the player takes on a first-person role in a realistic or science fiction scenario, and the object of the game is to destroy opponents by shooting them.

As these examples indicate, the very nature of video games is to be realistic, often three-dimensional representations of the world in which the game takes place, and the player is an interactive participant. This realism, which draws players into the game in a way that watching a movie or reading a book cannot, is a key reason behind the strong opinions voiced on all sides of the issue. Very few would disagree that playing video games can have a major impact on children. The disagreements revolve around the type and character of this impact, whether it be a help or a hindrance to children's education and growth.

The viewpoints in *Opposing Viewpoints: Video Games* largely relate to the influence video games have on young people. Most of the viewpoints are written by digital immigrants, who attempt to navigate a world that is unfamiliar to them while maintaining their roles as a conduit of learning from one generation to the next. The chapters are titled "What Effect Do Video Games Have on Children and Teens?" "How Do Video Games Affect Society?" "What Is the Impact of Violence in Video Games?" and "How Should Video Games Be Regulated?" The viewpoints in the following chapters explore the challenges faced by both adults and young people as they attempt to find safe and healthy ways to live and learn in the twenty-first century.

What Effect Do Video Games Have on Children and Teens?

Chapter Preface

On August 3, 2005, a young South Korean man in his twenties named Lee Seung Seop played a video game, *StarCraft*, at an Internet café for almost fifty hours, with only minimal breaks to eat or sleep. His friends found him on the third day suffering from exhaustion and dehydration. He soon collapsed, was taken to the hospital, and died, presumably of heart failure. His friends said he was addicted to gaming and had recently been fired from his job because he had missed work so he could play games. Lee is an extreme example, illustrating the dangers of excessive video gaming.

In 2007, an American Medical Association committee recommended that the group "strongly encourage the consideration and inclusion of 'Internet/video game addiction' as a formal diagnostic disorder in the upcoming revision of the *Diagnostic and Statistical Manual of Mental Disorders*." The recommendation sparked heated debate as to whether frequent gaming can or cannot be considered an addiction. No conclusion was reached, and the originating committee referred the recommendation to the American Psychiatric Association instead.

Professionals and parents alike are concerned about the potential for video game addiction in children. Some believe that video games, by their very nature, cause addiction. Others contend that repetition of a pleasurable activity is not necessarily addiction. They believe that most people can play games without the activity detracting from other aspects of their lives.

In this chapter, the viewpoints examine various ways in which video games affect children. Topics of discussion include addiction and time use, whether video games are helpful or detrimental to learning, and the effects of video games on physical activity and obesity in children.

> "Can you learn, in a game, real-life
> things like finding your way around an
> offshore oil platform, trading financial
> instruments, managing a theme park,
> or being stealthy? You bet you can."

Video Games Help
Children Learn

Marc Prensky

*Marc Prensky is a speaker, author, and consultant in the areas of
education and learning. Much of his work deals specifically with
the connection between video games and learning. In the following viewpoint, Prensky describes five levels of learning that happen in video and computer games and explains how each level
relates to real-life learning. He calls the five levels* how, what,
why, where, *and* whether.

As you read, consider the following questions:

1. What skills does the author say people in the military
   can learn by playing video and computer games?

2. What does Prensky believe players learn about culture in
   the *where* level?

3. Does Prensky believe that violent games lead kids to commit violent acts?

In my view, there are five levels at which learning happens in video and computer games. I call them "How," "What," "Why," "Where," and "Whether." Let's take a look at each one in turn.

Learning Level 1: How

The most explicit kind of learning in video and computer games is how to do something. As you play you learn, gradually or quickly, the moves of the game—how the various characters, pieces, or anything else operate and what you can make them do. You learn how to drag tiles to build up a virtual city or theme park. You learn how to virtually fight and protect yourself. You learn how to train a creature and make it evolve. And of course you learn the physical manipulations of the controllers involved in doing all this.

Can you learn, in a game, real-life things like finding your way around an offshore oil platform, trading financial instruments, managing a theme park, or being stealthy? You bet you can. And gamers often choose their games because they are interested in learning these things.

An additional, unconscious "how" message you learn playing a game is that you control what happens on the screen, unlike when watching movies or TV. Even infants quickly learn this and sit fascinated, moving the mouse and watching the screen with glee for long periods. This is "real world" learning.

The way you learn to do these things depends mainly on the game's control mechanism. With the mouse and keyboard, or the typical console controller (two hands, several buttons), a player is not going to be doing much that physically resembles real life—the learning is mostly mental. But many game controllers, especially in arcades, are extremely lifelike.

The exact controls of a vehicle, the playing surfaces of a musical instrument, the remote surgery tools of a doctor, can all be used to control electronic games. On a recent visit to a Tokyo game arcade, I played various video games controlled by fire hoses, dog leashes, drums, guns, bicycles, hammers, typewriter keyboards, punching bags, cars, tambourines, telephones, train controls, kayak paddles, bus controls, maracas, a pool cue, and even a sushi chef's knife. In many of these games any border between game and real-life learning disappears entirely.

How do we know the learning at the "How" level actually takes place? Because we can observe it. People who practice something over and over typically get better at it.

Learning Level 2: What

At the second level, players learn *what* to do in any particular game (and, equally important, what not to do). In other words they learn the rules. One finds out by playing, for example, whether the rules of a shooting game allow you to attack a player on your own team, or whether a simulation game allows you to do destructive (or self-destructive) acts.

Most non-electronic games require that players learn at least some of the rules before starting. In electronic games, however, the rules are built in to the programming, and you learn them by trial and error as you play. In addition, players can typically change the built-in rules by using easily found codes known, to the dismay and misunderstanding of adults, as "cheat codes"—which are passed around from player to player via magazines, the Web, and word of mouth. What these codes really do is alter the games' rules by giving players extra weapons, lives, power, etc. So game players learn that rules aren't necessarily fixed, but can be altered. Is this a real-life lesson? How often do we hear business books exhorting managers to "change the rules of the game?"

Game players are constantly comparing the rules of whatever game they are playing to what they have learned elsewhere, asking themselves "Are the rules of this game fair and accurate in terms of what I know about the world?" We know this comparison happens because games with wildly unfair or inaccurate rules get quickly identified as "bogus" and don't get played much. If the rules of *Sim City*, for example, allowed a player to build a modern metropolis without electricity, no one would play it.

And players of all ages often argue heatedly about whether game rules reflect the "real world" in terms of physics ("What is the true trajectory of a missile in space?"), biology ("Could a person really sustain that hit and live?"), and human behavior ("Would an opponent actually do or say that?")

So the rules of video and computer games force a player, no matter what his or her age, to reflect—at least subconsciously—and compare the game to what they already know about life. This is important, "real-life" learning.

Kids learn about yet another aspect of rules at the What level: "What if we break them?" Players can be heard shouting "That's not fair!" or "You can't do that!" at a very early game-playing age, and this is precisely what they are learning about.

Learning Level 3: Why

Strategy—the *why* of a game—depends on, and flows from, the rules.

Successful game players learn that sometimes you need to attack openly, and other times stealthily. In some situations you need to hoard and be selfish, in others you need to cooperate. Complex moves are more effective than simple ones. Weak pieces gain power when used as a group. Keep your guard up, be prepared, and don't attack until you have the forces required. And be sure to reserve some of your resources for defense.

Game strategy (and tactics) are chock full of such lessons about "real life." Like the rules, a game's strategy needs to be life-like for a game to make sense. Again, players are always making unconscious comparisons. They know from life, for example, that a hierarchy of strength among species typically depends on size. If a smaller character can defeat a bigger one, they know he'd better have something—strength, endurance, weapons, spells—that makes him more powerful.

And now that single player games are quickly being supplanted by games that are multiplayer and networked, learning a computer or video game's "strategy" increasingly comprises learning to deal with other people, which is about as real-world as you can get.

Military officers have known for millennia that games can teach strategy, and the U.S. military is far ahead of the curve in using video and computer games for teaching. The U.S. Army, Air Force, Navy, and Marines all use video and computer games for learning skills ranging from squad-based teamwork, to flying, to safety, to submarining, and even to commanding units and multi-branch forces. The military now takes it for granted that its pilot candidates have mastered every military flight simulator game there is. What they expect is that these people have learned not so much *how* to fly a plane, but *why*—what are the strategies for fighting with one.

The same goes for submarines, tanks, and special forces, as well as business and sports. Here are some more of the strategic "why" lessons that are learned from playing computer and video games:

- Cause and effect
- Long term winning versus short term gains
- Order from seeming chaos
- Second-order consequences
- Complex system behaviors
- Counter-intuitive results

- Using obstacles as motivation
- The value of persistence.

Learning Level 4: Where

The "Where" level is the *context* level, which encompasses the huge amount of cultural and environmental learning that goes on in video and computer games. At this level players learn about the world of the game and the values it represents. They learn to handle cultural relativity, and to deal with different people and roles. They learn that on one planet, in one society, in one world you can't do X, even though it may be perfectly normal somewhere else. They learn their culture's ideas about achievement and leadership. They learn, for example, that although enemies may be hard to beat, if you persevere and learn enough, you can defeat them and win the game.

Games also reflect our values. Like most of American society, most of our computer and video games are not violent, and reflect, rather, our wide range of interests.

And finally, like all other forms of expression, video and computer games reflect and interpret the particular subculture(s) in which they are created. Although rarely given the credit and respect they deserve, the designers and builders of computer, and video games are, according to the highly respected scientist Danny Hillis, among the most intelligent and creative people in the world. The games they create reflect their own thoughts, fantasies, heroes and villains. Game players learn to identify with the game characters and with the cultures they inhabit.

How do we know this learning happens? Again, by observation. I've watched young kids fight over who gets to be "Link," the hero of the Nintendo *Zelda* games. Link is their hero, the "person" they want to be. The qualities he possesses—courage, the desire to search, explore, overcome all enemies and get to the end to save the princess—are the ones they want to possess. Of course other players may choose "Duke Nukem" as their hero. For better or for worse, kids use video and computer games as a filter through which to understand their lives, just as in the past they used stories (e.g. "You be Lancelot—I'll be Mordred"). But one big difference between games and stories is that kids learn *they can control* their hero's life, and not just in their fantasies.

Learning Level 5: Whether

The "Whether" level is where game players learn to make value-based and moral decisions—decisions about whether doing something is right or wrong. This level also includes the unconscious emotional messages that influence these decisions. It is therefore the most controversial of the learning levels. And it is the level where players can "really" win or lose their games, in terms of learning.

Learning at the *whether* level is created not only from amplification and reduction of certain elements, but also from the use of allegory and symbols. It comes from images, situations, sounds, music, and other emotion-producing effects being manipulated into powerful combinations, just as in a novel or movie. Learning at this level also comes from the rewards, punishments, and consequences in the game.

Certainly the combination of amplification, emotional cues, and rewards in certain fighting games lead players to learn that the answer to "Is it OK to kill this character in the game context?" is "Yes." But the important question is: Are kids also learning this about "real-life?" Do they leave these games with the message "This behavior is fun in a game," or with the message "I've got to run out and do this?" Do they generalize all their games' "whether" messages to the actual world they live in, or do they accept and retain some messages ("fighting is tough") and reject others ("everybody is an enemy")?

Learning Principles Are Seen in Electronic Games

Here are just a few (there are many more) of the learning principles that the player is (however tacitly) exposed to in learning to play these games:

• Learning is based on situated practice, not lectures and words out of context;

• There are lowered consequences for failure and taking risks (you've saved the game and can start over);

• Learning is a form of extended engagement of self as an extension of an identity to which the player is committed;

• The learner can customize the game to suit his or her style of learning;

• Problems are ordered so that the first ones to be solved in the game lead to fruitful generalizations about how to solve more complex problems later on;

• Explicit verbal information is given "just in time," when the player can make use of it, or "on demand," when the player feels ready for it and a need for it;

• Learning is interactive (the player acts on the game and the game acts back, allowing the player continually to test hypotheses and gain immediate feedback);

• There are multiple routes to solving a problem;

• There are intrinsic rewards (within the game) keyed to any player's level of expertise; . . .

The Elder Scrolls III: Morrowind and Learning. *Rockville, MD: Bethesda Softworks, 2002, p.113.*

I believe that, unless already severely disturbed, kids don't leave violent games with the message "I've got to run out and do this," at least not in our society. We've all fantasized about doing terrible harm to someone who's hurt us in some way, but very few of us actually follow through. Just as with the rules, game players are constantly cross-checking messages in the game, automatically and unconsciously—and occasionally consciously as well—and comparing the game's messages with whatever else they know or have heard. Messages that are consistent get accepted, messages that aren't get further examination. "We typically test media representations against our direct experience," says Henry Jenkins, professor of Comparative Media at MIT [Massachusetts Institute of Technology], "and dismiss them when they don't ring true."

We must, of course, watch out for our very youngest children, who have the most trouble sorting and discriminating. Still, as my game designer friend Noah Falstein reminds us, "We have to be careful about buying the rhetoric of people who blame the game *Doom* for Columbine and ignore the fact that those guys were building pipe bombs in their garage and their parents never noticed." There will always be kids who do not get society's message from their parents or elsewhere. But they are the exception.

The comparison of the "whether" learning in the game with the "whether" learning in the rest of life is the reason that shooting games can teach kids how to aim, without their learning to kill. To truly "learn" the latter, a player would have to have to overcome an awful lot of disconnects with the messages he or she hears in the rest of life.

It is certainly in our public interest to keep such countermessages as frequent and strong as possible. But although some critics argue that there should always be bad consequences for bad acts in games, most players would tell you that if games turned purely into moral lessons they would no longer be fun. Much of the appeal of many games, as well as other forms of entertainment, is "transgression in safety." Yet even this contains learning. "In recent years, [games] have tried to offer more morally complex and emotionally demanding representation of aggression, loss and suffering," says Jenkins. Those are important "real-life" emotions that all kids need to learn more about.

"GPA [grade point average] was lower in those who played video games for more than one hour. Even though this study cohort had a relatively high over-all GPA, the difference between an 'A' (less than one hour of video games) versus a 'B' (more than one hour of video games) is a significant change in grade."

Playing Video Games Causes Poor Grades

Philip A. Chan and Terry Rabinowitz

Philip A. Chan and Terry Rabinowitz are contributors to Annals of General Psychiatry. *The following viewpoint discusses their study, which mainly focused on the relationship between video game use and symptoms of attention deficit hyperactivity disorder (ADHD) and poor grades among high school students. The study concluded that playing video games for more than one hour per day resulted in negative impacts on both the social lives of the students and their academic performance.*

Philip A. Chan and Terry Rabinowitz, "A Cross-sectional Analysis of Video Games and Attention Deficit Hyperactivity Disorder Symptoms in Adolescents," *Annals of General Psychiatry*, vol. 5, October, 2006, pp. 1–2, 4–5, 10. Copyright © 2006 Chan and Rabinowicz; licensee BioMed Central Ltd. Reproduced by permission.

As you read, consider the following questions:

1. What is the difference between a console game and Internet games?

2. What does the YIAS-VG measure? According to the authors, what does an increase in YIAS-VG scores imply?

3. According to the authors, what is it about video games that causes the "time dependent relationship" between video games and behavior disorders?

The introduction of the telegraph in the nineteenth century ushered in a new era of communication and social development. Further advances in technology led to the creation of the telephone, radio, and television. Recently, the Internet has become the pinnacle of interchange in the modern world and facilitates many different modes of communication. Each generation has raised concerns regarding the negative impact of media on social skills and personal relationships. The Internet appeals to adolescents for many reasons and has become a social connection for many with uses including messaging, e-mail, gaming, education, and music.

Video Games and Adolescents

The Internet and other media types are reported to have important social and mental health effects in adolescents. The association between television viewing and obesity, attention disorders, school performance, and violence has been reported. Likewise, recent studies on obsessive Internet use called "Internet Addiction" have shown negative effects on social health. A significant relationship between Internet use and attention deficit hyperactivity disorder (ADHD) has also been shown in elementary school children. Other studies have reported the similarities between computer video game addiction and pathological gambling or substance dependence.

The effect of video games on adolescents is not well characterized despite a growing body of evidence demonstrating their addictive nature and popularity. Indeed, video game use may exceed that of television use in children. In pre-adolescent teenagers, obesity has been linked to increasing time spent on video games, but other studies have disputed this finding in different populations. Most studies of mental health and media use did not specifically examine video games, but included them as a subset of television or Internet use. One extensively studied area is the content of video games and their relationship to subsequent aggressive behavior in children. Other case reports have documented associations between video games and various conditions such as epilepsy, musculoskeletal disorders, and deep vein thrombosis, although the strength of these associations has not yet been established.

The Difference Between Console and Internet Games

The term "video-games" does not always differentiate between console and Internet/computer video games but instead, suggests a loose clustering. Console video games include Nintendo, Sony Playstation, Microsoft Xbox, and others. Internet video games refer to computer games played online in a community setting with other players. Although similar in nature, several important differences exist. Console games can be played with other people, but most games are "single player" and are meant to be played alone. Internet games, however, are designed for "multi-player" use and are played with others online, usually at distant sites. Console games are less expensive than Internet games, and do not require a computer. The genre of video games played on the Internet versus console games also differs in content. Console game themes include sports, action, strategy, family, puzzle, role-playing games, and simulation, while video game themes designed for Internet use are more specific and are mainly action and strategy. The video game market, regardless of type, is a multi-billion dollar industry that generally targets children and adolescents.

Video Games and ADHD

The relationship between video games and ADHD is unknown. The incidence of ADHD continues to rise and is a significant challenge on medical, financial, and educational resources. ADHD is a complex disorder that often requires input from the affected child or adolescent, teachers, parents, and physicians in order to be diagnosed correctly and treated successfully. The Conners' Parent Rating Scale (CPRS) is the most widely used instrument to aid in the diagnosis of children with ADHD. The CPRS comprises both a parent and teacher questionnaire, and includes a number of components including oppositional behavior, hyperactivity, inattention, and ADHD.

This study examined the relationship between video game use and symptoms of ADHD. Other parameters studied included body mass index (BMI), school grades, work, detentions, and family situation.

After receiving IRB approval, subjects were recruited from a local high school in Vermont. Permission from school officials was obtained and contact was made with the guidance office and school teachers. Surveys were distributed to all 9th and 10th grade students at the school. The survey included sections for students (five pages) and parents (two pages) to complete independently, as well as a consent form which needed to be signed by both the student and parent for participation in the study. All survey data was anonymous. Surveys were collected through the school Guidance Office.

ADHD among children and adolescents has been attributed to both genetic and environmental factors. Of the media influences, only excessive Internet use has been reported to be associated with ADHD. The diagnosis of ADHD relies on input from teachers, parents, and physicians. This study found an increase in ADHD and inattention symptoms in adolescents who play video games for more than one hour a day.

The prevalence of ADHD in adolescents is reported to be 4–7%. This study found a prevalence of 8.3% based on a reported diagnosis by a parent. It was not possible to determine the actual diagnosis of ADHD based only on the raw scores of the CPRS. More or more severe symptoms of inattention and ADHD behavior were found in students who played video games for more than one hour, but further study is needed to more clearly understand the association between video games and ADHD. It is unclear whether playing video games for more than one hour leads to an increase in ADHD symptoms, or whether adolescents with ADHD symptoms spend more time on video games.

Social and Academic Effects

Both console and Internet video games were associated with an increase in addiction scores as measured by YIAS-VG. The YIAS-VG assesses the degree to which video games negatively impact different social factors including daily activities, relationships, sleep, and daily thoughts. The increase in YIAS-VG scores imply that playing video games for more than one hour a day does have a negative impact on relationships and daily activity. We did not define a cutoff on the YIAS-VG to identify "excessive" video game use but the scores in our cohort were not high enough to be considered as evidence of "Internet Addiction".

GPA [grade point average] was lower in those who played video games for more than one hour. Even though this study cohort had a relatively high overall GPA, the difference between an "A" (less than one hour of video games) versus a "B" (more than one hour of video games) is a significant change in grade. For students who are less academically proficient, this may be especially important. There was also a trend towards a lower GPA in students who watch television for more than one hour. Excessive television has been reported to be associated with poor school performance.

Video Gaming Hinders Performance in School

Students' performance in school is negatively affected by video gaming. Generally, the percentage of students who report excellent performance decreases with increased screen time, and the reports of below average performance increase.

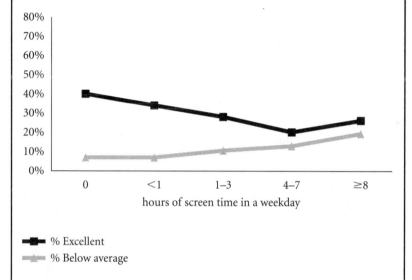

hours of screen time in a weekday

■ % Excellent
▲ % Below average

TAKEN FROM: Iman Sharif and James D. Sargent, "Association Between Television, Movie, and Video Game Exposure and School Performance," *Pediatrics*, October 2006.

This investigation found that playing console and Internet video games for more than one hour a day has negative social and academic effects in adolescents. This association does not depend on being "addicted" to video games or playing for excessive time periods. Furthermore, there was no difference between playing video games on the Internet or on a console system. The intensive nature of video games is likely to cause this time dependent relationship between video games and behavior disorders, regardless of whether it is over the Internet or on a console system.

To our knowledge, this is the first study to find an association between video game use and ADHD symptoms in adolescents. Assessment of ADHD risk factors often involves identification of home and academic environmental factors. Parental relationships, early childhood development factors (i.e. preterm delivery), and excessive Internet use are associated with ADHD later in life. Identification of these and other risk factors that contribute to ADHD will lead to prevention and earlier treatment strategies.

> "The empty pursuit of game points, levels, adventure, sex, conquest, and domination ends up replacing meaningful goals by draining all desire for the life-renewing, God-given passions of real life."

Video Gaming Is a Waste of Time

Olivia Bruner and Kurt Bruner

Kurt and Olivia Bruner are authors and speakers on the subject of video game addiction, and they host the Web site Video GameTrouble.org. *In this viewpoint, an excerpt from their book* Playstation Nation: Protect Your Child from Video Game Addiction, *they discuss how time spent playing video games prevents young people, especially boys, from achieving their real-life potential.*

As you read, consider the following questions:

1. How does John Messerly say that students try to make money from games?

2. Do the authors believe that boys or girls are more seriously in danger of video game addiction?

3. How do the Bruners describe the idea of manhood that has emerged from the video game culture?

Some might expect young men who have limited skills or opportunities to spend an excessive amount of time playing games as a means of replacing a thrill-less existence. But a growing percentage of society's best and brightest, those who should see the world as their oyster, are sacrificing their real-life potential in order to beat the next level of a game.

John Messerly, lecturer at the Department of Computer Sciences at the University of Texas at Austin, provides a snapshot of the problem. He conducted interviews with more than a thousand students about their gaming habits in order to confirm his suspicion that game addiction was diminishing the potential of otherwise gifted young people, particularly among computer science majors. Messerly's conclusions should cause concern for any parent doling out thousands of dollars for tuition, books, room, and board in order to give their kids the opportunities afforded by a college education.

Knowing students might "sugarcoat" the reality of video game addiction, Messerly decided to ask whether they "know someone" whose social or scholastic life had been negatively affected by these games. More than 90 percent said that they did, describing "friends" who remained chained to their dorm room or apartment for days, weeks, even semesters.

Role-Playing Games Encourage Escape

Role-playing games like *EverQuest* emerge as particularly problematic among those questioned. The big allure, they admit, is escapism. "One can live in these virtual worlds," explains Messerly, "with little or no interaction with the ordinary world right now." Many students admitted that real life offers less interesting options than the exciting universes found in their

A Student Describes How Gaming Led to Failure

There are times when being a college student can be overwhelming. By turning to video games so much, you really do lose self-esteem and confidence that you can face adversities in life and be successful. It is a very vicious cycle. When you don't succeed or live up to your expectations, all of a sudden it's reinforcing the cycle because you go back to the video games to escape your sense of failure. It's just easier.

My freshman year I lived in the dorms, and I did really badly in school. When I came back to school in my sophomore year, I lived in a house with two other guys. I was really committed to getting back on track and working hard. I thought that a lot of the problems I had—playing video games, my sleep cycle, and my overall health—were problems because I lived in the dorms, around so many people who played all the time. I thought just living with two other guys would end that, but it didn't. One of the guys went out and bought a big-screen TV, and that's what we did when we weren't in class, which was most of the time. We were in front of the TV, either watching it or playing video games. It caught up with me, and I couldn't get rid of the problem. . . . I started off that semester on probation and I failed out of school. I moved down to my dad's house in Albuquerque, where I am right now. When I came down here, I said, "Okay, that's it," and I got rid of the video games. It was really easier to do once I was by myself. I decided I was going to get my life back on track.

Olivia Bruner and Kurt Bruner, Playstation Nation: Protect Your Child from Video Game Addiction, *New York: Center Street, 2006, p. 66.*

games. In fact, when confronted with the possibility that Mom and Dad might not want to fund their student "wasting" time on games instead of studies, some say it is even possible to derive a living from role-playing computer games.

"Evidently," Messerly explains, "gamers create and develop characters—a time-consuming process—and sell them for profit."

I met with one such student who seemed especially pleased with his own entrepreneurial initiative for selling one such character, listing it as justification for the hundreds of hours invested. When I asked how much he had earned while wasting his parents' tuition money, he sheepishly acknowledged it was less than a hundred dollars. He laughed at himself when I pointed out that earning a few pennies per hour is hardly a promising career! But as Messerly reveals, the tendency of students to justify their time on such games continues, especially among those pursuing computer science degrees.

"As for the claim that some gaming is needed for computer science education," affirms Messerly, "I simply reject it." It's an important observation from someone who teaches computer science at the university level.

Messerly compares video games to cigarette addiction, saying those who smoke feel a need for and perceive benefits from their habit. After all, if you take away the cigarettes, they feel even greater stress due to withdrawal. His conclusion?

"Similarly, role-playing games may appear good to those playing—because they want to escape the world or are afraid of it—but for the moment the real world holds much more for those who have the courage to face it. It holds more depth, more possible experience, more knowledge, more joy, more beauty, and more love than the world of a computer-generated reality. It is possible to imagine that in the future this may no longer be the case; but for the present such escapism is cowardly."

Young Men Are the Most Vulnerable

In the conclusion of his report, Messerly observes that the problem of video game addiction appears most serious among young men. He notes that these games target "primal areas of the brain" and satisfy "primitive needs in the (primarily male) psyche." This observation is consistent with every other study I've encountered that suggests boys and men are far more likely to become hooked than girls. . . . Many of the games are intentionally designed with elements that play to the basic drives of the male psyche, including adventure, competition, and desire for mastery.

The teachings of my Christian faith compel men to follow the model of Jesus Christ, who said that we must lose our life to find it, and that the greatest love is to lay one's life down for another. In other words, we discover true meaning in life through self-sacrifice, not self-gratification. For men, that means finding fulfillment through the sacrificial love of marriage and fatherhood and/or building something that can contribute to the good of others. By disciplining their strengths and skills and investing in the lives of others, men play their God-ordained role in the world.

The contrast to young men investing their lives in video games couldn't be starker or sadder, because it meets those basic drives of manhood in an artificial manner that is self-focused rather than others-focused. The empty pursuit of game points, levels, adventure, sex, conquest, and domination ends up replacing meaningful goals by draining all desire for the life-renewing, God-given passions of real life.

A very different idea of manhood has emerged over the past two decades due to the video game culture. As Tom Chiarella commented after meeting Suicide Bob [leader of a tribe of gamers], "There's a subset of manhood in America: adult males who are forgoing ambition, sex, money, love, adventure to sit in darkened rooms mastering video games."

Boys are preprogrammed to find fulfillment as men who build something that will improve society. Video game addiction is causing men to remain boys, building nothing more than a high score. They show little evidence of industry, self-discipline, or desire to make their world a better place.

| *"All of us can use games to learn how to function in the era of continuous partial attention."*

Video Games Help Children Learn Time Management Skills

Henry Jenkins

Henry Jenkins is the director of the Massachusetts Institute of Technology Comparative Media Studies Program and the author of numerous books and articles on media and popular culture. In this viewpoint, he asserts that multitasking is an important time management skill in the current technological age and that playing video games is an effective way to learn multitasking skills.

As you read, consider the following questions:

1. What style of learning does the author say classic notions of literacy assume?

2. Pointing out that those in earlier civilizations used play to improve hunting skills, what does Jenkins say can be enhanced by computer games?

3. Besides playing games, what else does the author believe is necessary to produce children who have a balanced perspective?

Frank Lantz, the head of game design at New York GameLab, demonstrated *Arcadia* at the Game Developers Conference a few years back. Astonishingly, Lantz played four basic Atari-style games on the screen at the same time. In one window, he was arranging puzzle pieces. In another, he was making a funny little man run through a scrolling maze. In another, he was defending the Earth against alien invaders. And in a fourth, he was moving his paddle to deflect a *Pong* ball. His mouse circled between windows, always seeming to be in the right place at the right time to avert disaster or grab an enticing power-up. Each game created a different spatial orientation—in and out, up and down, right and left. To anyone who respects skilled game play, Lantz gave a virtuoso performance.

As Lantz played, Eric Zimmerman, GameLab's cofounder and resident game theorist, offered explanations for what we were seeing, demonstrating the fusion of insightful and innovative design that has been the group's hallmark. The folks at GameLab create games that make you think about the nature of the medium. I want to use their provocation to explore some key questions at the intersection of games, attention, and learning.

Playing a Game That Includes Four Games at Once

I am old enough to have played *Pong* and to have spent whole evenings mastering some of those Atari games when they first appeared. Those games used to be hard. Now, gamers like Lantz can handle four of them at a time and not break a sweat. What happened?

When I spoke to him by telephone, Zimmerman reassured me that there was a trick—the games had been simplified and slowed down from the originals. As soon as any one game got interesting enough that you wanted to play it on its own, it was probably too complicated for *Arcadia*. Yet, when I tried to play *Arcadia*, even on its easiest setting, I found myself constantly losing lives, frantically racing from place to place, and always, always, always arriving too late. To use a technical term, I sucked. *Arcadia* is set to launch at Shockwave.com in early August [2003], so you can see how you stack up.

GameLab works outside the mainstream industry, designing games for the Web, not for the PC or the various game machines. Zimmerman, who recently finished a book, *Rules of Play*, with Katie Salen, sees each game as an experiment in interactive engineering. Much as punk rockers tried to strip rock music down to its core, GameLab embraces a minimalist retro aesthetic, shedding fancy graphics to focus on the mechanics of game play. In one of its games, *Loop*, there aren't even mouse clicks: you simply encircle butterflies by moving your mouse across the screen. Another GameLab title, *Sissyfight 2000*, was a staging of *Prisoner Dilemma* as a multiplayer game set in a schoolyard. All of the emphasis is on social interactions—the choice to tattle, tease, bond with or abuse your classmates.

Arcadia began as a game about minigames—small, simple games that are increasingly embedded within larger and more complicated games. It evolved into a game about multitasking, one that links the management of game resources with the management of one's own attention. That's actually a core issue for many of us right now—how to manage our perceptual and cognitive resources in what digital community builder Linda Stone characterizes as an age of continuous partial attention.

Stone argues that there is a growing tendency for people to move through life, scanning their environments for signals, and shifting their attention from one problem to another. This process has definite downsides—we never give ourselves over

"We're very worried that John's homework has started to interfere with his computer gaming." Cartoon by NAF. www.Cartoonstock.com.

fully to any one interaction. It is like being at a cocktail party and constantly looking over the shoulders of the person you are talking with to see if anyone more interesting has arrived. Yet, it is also adaptive to the demands of the new information environment, allowing us to accomplish more, to sort through competing demands, and to interact with a much larger array of people.

Multitasking Is Second Nature to Teens and Twentysomethings

For my generation, this process feels highly stressful and socially disruptive. But for my son's cohort, young men and women in their late teens or early twenties, it has become second nature. I am amazed watching my son doing his homework, chatting online with multiple friends, each in their own chat room window, downloading stuff off the Web, listening to MP3s, and keeping an eye on the Red Sox score. My parents couldn't understand how I could do homework and watch television. My students sit in class discussions, take detailed notes, and look up relevant Web sites on their wireless laptops.

Our classic notions of literacy assume uninterrupted contemplation in relative social isolation, a single task at a time. Some have characterized the younger generation as having limited attention spans. But these young people have also developed new competencies at rapidly processing information, forming new connections between separate spheres of knowledge, and filtering a complex field to discern those elements that demand immediate attention. Stone argues that for better or worse, this is the way we are all currently living. Therefore, she claims, we had better design our technologies to accommodate continuous partial attention, and we had better evolve forms of etiquette that allow us to smooth over the social disruptions such behavior can cause.

Contemporary aesthetic choices—the fragmented, MTV-style editing, the dense layering of techno music, the more visually complex pages of some contemporary comic books—reflect consumers' desires for new forms of perceptual play and their capacity to take in more information at once than previous generations. Think for a moment about the scrawl—the layering of informational windows—in today's TV news. Like *Arcadia*'s minigames, there is a trick: any given bit of text is simplified compared to previous news discourse. Such graphical busyness also has an advantage—we can see the interrelationship between stories and pay attention to simultaneous developments. We probably don't read everything on screen, but we monitor and flit between different media flows.

Video Game Play Improves Perceptual and Cognitive Skills

All of this brings us back to games like *Arcadia*. Much as earlier civilizations used play to sharpen their hunting skills, we use computer games to exercise and enhance our information processing capabilities. Researchers at the University of Rochester found that kids who regularly play intense video games show better perceptual and cognitive skills than those who do not. It isn't just that people who had quick eyes and nimble fingers liked to play games; these skills could be acquired by non-gamers who put in the time and effort to learn how to play.

Zimmerman argues that what makes playing *Arcadia* possible is the degree to which each of the minigames builds on conventions. We take one look at these games and we know what to do. Yet, the Rochester research suggests something else—that people over time simply become quicker at processing game information and can play more sophisticated games. In a new book, *What Video Games Can Teach Us About Learning and Literacy*, James Paul Gee argues that games are, in some senses, the ideal teaching machines. Gee suggests that educators can learn a great deal about how to sequence a curriculum from watching how game designers orient players to new challenges and how they organize the flow of activities so that players acquire the skills they need just in time for the next task; the goal is for players to find each level challenging but not overwhelming. Games teach us, Gee argues, without us even realizing that any education is taking place.

All of this research points in the same direction. Leaving aside questions of content, video games are good for kids—within limits—because game play helps them to adapt to the demands of the new information environment. Surgeons are already using video games to refine their hand-eye coordination for the ever more exacting demands of contemporary procedures. The military uses games to rehearse the complexity of coordinating group actions in an environment where participants cannot see each other. And all of us can use games to learn how to function in the era of continuous partial attention.

These multitasking skills will be most developed in those who have had access to games from an early age. Our sons and daughters will be the natives of the new media environment; others will be immigrants. Educators have long talked about a hidden curriculum, things kids absorb outside of formal education that shape their thoughts, tastes, and skills and that enable some groups to advance more quickly than others. The same pattern is developing around new media technologies—those who grow up with them as part of their recreational life relate to them differently than those who only encounter them later at school or work.

While the skills derived from playing video games expand human creative capacity and broaden access to knowledge, they should not come at the expense of older forms of literacy. The challenge is to produce children who have a balanced perspective—who know what each medium does best and what kind of content is most appropriate in each, who can multitask but can also contemplate, who play games but also read books.

So, get thee to *Arcadia* but also get thee to a library.

> *"Concern is spreading among parents and mental-health professionals that the exploding popularity of computer and video games has a deeper dark side than simple couch-potatohood."*

Addiction to Video Gaming Is a Problem

Jennifer Seter Wagner

In the following viewpoint, reporter Jennifer Seter Wagner highlights growing concerns among parents and mental health professionals about the potentially addictive qualities of computer and video games. She cites an Iowa State University study that indicates that 8.5 percent of teen gamers can be considered addicted. The viewpoint also cautions parents to be aware of a number of behaviors that may be warning signs of addiction. Wagner contends that although gaming addiction is not currently recognized by the American Psychiatric Association as a mental disorder, it falls under a broader category of "behavioral addictions." She discusses how gaming addiction is being treated in several places around the world.

Jennifer Seter Wagner, "When Play Turns to Trouble," *U.S. News & World Report*, vol. 144, May 19, 2008, pp. 51–53. Copyright © 2008 U.S. News and World Report, L.P. All rights reserved. Reprinted with permission.

As you read, consider the following questions:

1. What percentage of children under eighteen does the author say play computer or video games regularly?

2. What type of games does the author believe is most likely to be overplayed?

3. What addiction does Keith Bakker of the Smith and Jones Center in Amsterdam compare gaming to?

Ollie Morelli, 7, logs on to the family laptop before sunup to make sure his pet lion, Cedric, is set for the day. The character in the online game Webkinz would appear to be: His house, furnished by Ollie, boasts a football-shaped refrigerator, a football-helmet coffee table, a couch, and a flat-screen TV. Cedric requires hours of after-school attention, too—and sometimes inspires an outburst when Mom and Dad say, "Enough!" Like many parents these days, Ollie's have wondered uneasily where childish pastime begins to edge toward obsession. "The issue is not the amount of time," says Brian Morelli. "We can control that. It's the fact that he gets up before everyone else and sneaks onto the computer. It's like he sets his internal clock so he can play Webkinz."

Concern is spreading among parents and mental-health professionals that the exploding popularity of computer and video games has a deeper dark side than simple couch-potatohood. Software sales jumped 28 percent [in 2007] to $9.5 billion; an average of nine games were sold every second of the year, according to the Entertainment Software Association. Studies show that 92 percent of children under age 18 play regularly. According to the Media Research Lab at Iowa State University, about 8.5 percent of 8-to-18-year-old gamers can be considered pathologically addicted, and nearly one quarter of young people—more males than females—admit they've felt addicted. Little wonder: In February [2008], a team at Stanford University School of Medicine showed that areas of the brain responsible for generating feelings of addiction and reward are activated during game play. "We are seeing it over and over again," says Liz Woolley, founder of On-Line Gamers Anonymous (www.olganonboard.org), a virtual 12-step program for gaming addicts. "We're losing [kids] into the games, and it's turning their brains to mush."

Knowing How Much Is Too Much

How can parents know when a lot is too much? Media experts are quick to point out that computer and video games are not inherently bad for kids; indeed, most players find a balance, says David Walsh, founder of the National Institute on Media and the Family in Minneapolis: "They play their video games; they do their homework; they keep up with their responsibilities and have other interests. No problem."

But when the other areas of a child's life begin to suffer, parents may have cause to take corrective action. Kimberly Young, director of the Center for Internet Addiction Recovery in Bradford, Pa., points to several common warning signs of pathological behavior: fantasizing or talking about game characters or missions when offline; lying about or hiding how much time is spent playing or disobeying parental limits; losing interest in sports and hobbies; choosing the game over time with friends; and continuing to play despite plummeting grades, loss of a scholarship, a breakup with a partner. An addicted gamer's physical appearance may also change as he loses sleep, neglects to shower, and skips meals.

Team Pressure Encourages Addiction

The games most apt to be overplayed are what people in the industry call MMORPGs, or "massively multiplayer online role-playing games." Games of this type—*World of Warcraft* and *Call of Duty* are two popular examples—connect players in cyberspace who then form "guilds" or "clans" that participate in raids against opposing squads. Generally, each player is

Results of a National Study on Video Game Addiction

Using a national sample of youth aged 8 to 18, 8.5 percent of video game players exhibited pathological patterns of play as defined by exhibiting at least six out of eleven symptoms of damage to family, social, school, or psychological functioning. Although this may at first appear to be high, it is very similar to the prevalence demonstrated in many other studies of this age group, including across nations, such as a prevalence rate 9.9 percent of Spanish adolescents. . . . Pathological gamers compared to non-pathological gamers spent twice as much time playing games (24 hours/week), were more likely to have video game systems in their bedrooms, reported having more trouble paying attention at school, received poorer grades in school, had more health problems, and were more likely to feel "addicted.". . . Pathological gamers were not more likely to have televisions in their bedrooms, use the Internet for homework; nor was pathological status related significantly to age, race, or type of school attended. Pathological use (or "addiction") must mean more than 'do it a lot.' As predicted, pathological status was a significant predictor of poorer school performance even after controlling for sex, age, and weekly amount of video game play.

Douglas A. Gentile,
"Pathological Video Game Use Among Youth 8 to 18:
A National Study," Psychological Science, *September 22, 2008.*

represented by an avatar—usually a three-dimensional character that either the game or the player creates—and has a role to play, such as defender or strategist. Guild members may be from all over the world, and the missions can go on for days.

"Let's say I'm a ninth grader, with teammates in Japan and Bulgaria, and Mom says it's time to do homework," says Walsh. "I e-mail my teammates I need to stop, and their response is: 'Are you nuts?' The membership on the teams becomes very important to these kids. Dropping out of a mission is not OK." The longer you play, says Young, "the more you begin to identify with this make-believe world."

One mother and physician in the Midwest, who asked for anonymity to protect her son, is all too familiar with the siren call of the game. Her son, now 21, started playing computer games as a young child, graduated to *World of Warcraft* in high school, and spent so much time online as a college freshman that he got mostly F's and was forced to withdraw. His mom says that the progression from great kid and student to self-destructive abuser stupefied the family. "I didn't understand this was a whole different thing," she says of the game. "I'd call him to dinner, and he couldn't come," she says. "'We're in the middle of a raid!' he'd say. 'They need me!'"

Once he left college, he had to make a choice: either find somewhere else to live and play the game, at his expense, or quit the game, start working, and go back to school part time. He chose the latter and is now finishing up an associate's degree. "We determined there would be no computer games allowed in our house when we saw how destructive they could be," says his mother. The family even locked up the computers. "The longer he spends away from this, the more he'll realize how destructive and what a fantasy world it was," she says. "But I don't know what will happen when he goes out on his own."

Therapy wasn't an option, since the young man was an adult and refused to go. But even when age or willingness isn't an issue, finding effective professional help can be a challenge. For now, game addiction is not recognized by the American Psychiatric Association [APA], which means that there are no national guidelines for what therapy should entail. Whether this will change in 2012, the date a new APA handbook on mental disorders is scheduled to come out, is still up for discussion. Pathological video and computer game play would now be considered one of a broad group of "behavioral addictions" that also includes compulsive shopping and addiction to online pornography, for example. The only behavioral addiction now specifically listed in the handbook is pathological gambling. To treat these disorders, cognitive behavioral therapy is often used to identify the thought processes that lead to the compulsion and to change the destructive thinking. Families seeking help may need to pay out of their own pockets, because insurance typically doesn't cover addictions that don't officially exist. That said, many young gamers are diagnosed with other conditions such as depression or obsessive-compulsive disorder.

Getting Help for the Addiction

Elsewhere in the world, the problem is recognized as huge. Governments in China and South Korea have helped fund treatment centers and hotlines for electronic game addicts. Keith Bakker, director of the Smith and Jones Center in Amsterdam, a residential detox center that treats video game addicts from around the world, compares their poison to crack cocaine. But "it's easier to treat a coke addict than it is a gamer," he says. "The gamer's denial is so great, and it's compounded by family and community," he says. "Who in the world thinks gaming is a problem?" At first, the center kept gamers physically apart from other addicts, but results were much better when the kids took group therapy with residents troubled by eating disorders, marijuana, or cocaine. "They began to see the similarities between themselves," Bakker says. After they stop denying they have an addiction and the damage it's causing, he notes, many young people never pick up a game again.

In this country, some families are turning to wilderness therapy. The Aspen Education Group, a California-based organization that treats underachievers from around the country, provides young people ages 11 to 18 with a back-to-nature approach to ending their gaming obsessions. "At home when they have frustrations, they go to their video games," says therapist Aaron Shaw. "Here they have cold weather, hiking." By being away from their screens for seven to nine weeks, he says, "they learn some healthier coping mechanisms." Shaw first tries to discover kids' reasons for playing; often, he finds, it's to find freedom and fun and out of a need for greater acceptance from their parents. (If Mom is always nagging that games are a waste of time, notes Shaw, "they say: 'Screw you, my friends online love me, and I'll hang out with them.'")

To that point, Young advises parents who want to head off serious trouble to find ways to limit play without blaming or criticizing. Better to set—and enforce—time restrictions . . . put electronics in a well-trafficked area, and make it easy for a child to choose clubs or sports. Games should never be a child's main focus, cautions Woolley. Her wisdom is hard won. Several years ago, Woolley's son committed suicide in front of his computer with his favorite game on the screen.

> "Addictive drugs are dangerous because they alter the supply of neurotransmitters [dopamine] directly. Since we don't ingest videogames, they're limited in their immediate chemical power over the brain."

The Addictive Qualities of Video Games Are Not a Problem

Steven Johnson

Steven Johnson is a popular science author who has written a number of books and articles including Everything Bad Is Good for You. *In this viewpoint, Johnson gives his opinion about gaming as an addiction. He admits that the qualities of reward and exploration provided by video games trigger the neurotransmitter dopamine, a factor in drug addiction, to be released into the brain. Johnson contends, however, that dopamine is also present in many nonaddictive experiences such as studying hard to achieve good grades. He believes that as gaming becomes more integrated into popular culture, it will be considered a normal part of daily life instead of an addiction.*

As you read, consider the following questions:

1. What does neuroscientist Jaak Panksepp say are the evolutionary advantages of the "seeking circuitry" largely controlled by dopamine?

2. What does Johnson say is different between finishing a game of *Pac-Man* or *Myst* and playing games like *Ever-Quest?*

3. How soon will virtual avatars be as common as e-mail addresses, according to Johnson?

Early this August, [2005] a 28-year-old South Korean man died of heart failure after playing the computer game *Starcraft* for 50 straight hours. When the story hit the wires, you could almost hear all the parents of teenage gamers across the planet collectively shriek: "I told you so!"

Even the most ardent defenders of gaming culture—and I happen to be one—have to admit that videogames have an addictive power that is stronger than the siren songs of other media. You sit down to play *Halo* for a few minutes after dinner, and the next thing you know it's midnight. You find yourself daydreaming new strategies for your characters in *The Sims* while sitting through a meeting at work. Most of us manage to avoid the 50-hour marathons, of course, but even five straight hours of *Starcraft* is obsessive enough.

There's a neurological explanation for that addictiveness. The human brain is wired to respond strongly to situations that combine both the promise of reward and the exploration of new environments. The neuroscientist Jaak Panksepp, a professor emeritus at Bowling Green State University, calls this the "seeking circuitry" of the brain. Its evolutionary advantages are easy to understand: brains wired to search their environments for food or shelter or mates are more likely to survive and pass their genes on to the next generation. The seeking circuitry is largely controlled by the neurotransmitter dopamine, which also plays a crucial role in most addictive drugs.

Among all forms of popular entertainment, videogames are uniquely designed as hybrids of reward and exploration: you probe a virtual world, looking for a veritable treasure chest of prizes—access to new levels, new weapons, magic coins, special privileges. This is not the cognitive environment of movies or music or books—we don't "explore" these forms in anything but the more figurative sense of the word. Reward exploration is the defining experience of gaming, which means it is custom-tailored to attract the attention of the human brain. No wonder studies have shown that gameplay triggers dopamine release in the brain.

Games Are Not the Same as Crack Cocaine

Here's where we need to be careful. Noting the connection between dopamine and gameplay is not reason to assume that videogames are the digital version of crack cocaine. Addictive drugs are dangerous because they alter the supply of neurotransmitters directly. Since we don't ingest videogames, they're limited in their immediate chemical power over the brain. Besides, many life experiences that we cherish and encourage in our kids activate the dopamine system. The high-school honors student who works hard to earn that A and her parents' praise—her drive for intellectual reward is triggering dopamine release in her brain as well. On some basic level, that's what her drive is.

Right now, of course, the virtual rewards of gaming tend to be childish or violent, though a growing number of games offer more sophisticated pleasures. But as the gaming generation grows up—the average player is now 29—those rewards will become less fanciful and escapist in nature. Ten years from now the line between real life and games will have blurred significantly. Saying that someone is "addicted" to a

Dopamine in Everyday Situations

There is hardly a situation in which this substance doesn't play a role. There's some fresh fruit in the supermarket that at that moment happens to appeal to us—dopamine is released. We feel a surge of happiness, a joyful and excited "I want it!" Under the influence of dopamine, the brain gives orders to the muscles to stretch out the arm and reach for the apple. While the brain prepares to test whether the apple actually tastes as good as we had hoped, the ability to store memories is activated, enabling us to note for the future whether the experience was a good one or a disappointment.

Dopamine is involved when we attack a new problem at work, and when we pass an attractive person on the street, and, in a big way, when we anticipate sex. If we reach for a glass of beer or a cigarette, we're also looking for a pleasurable extra ration of this transmitter, for one of the main effects of alcohol and nicotine is to release more dopamine in the brain.

Stefan Klein, The Science of Happiness. *New York: Marlow & Company, 2002.*

game will sound as odd as saying someone is addicted to having friends, or keeping up with his extended family.

People spend so much time in multiplayer games like *Ever-Quest* and the burgeoning [online] communities of *There* and *Second Life* not because they want to finish the game the way my generation wanted to make it all the way to the end of *Pac-Man* or *Myst*, but because they've literally become part of the world in which they live; the fate of their own characters has become emotionally tied to their own fate as human beings. And because these spaces are where they've made some of their closest friends, even if they've never seen them face to face. In 10 years, the idea of having a virtual avatar will be almost as commonplace as having a virtual address (think e-mail) is today.

Will that mean that we're "addicted" to these online environments? No more so than many of us today are addicted to talking on the phone. We readily accept the idea that the phone is a legitimate channel of communication, even though it compresses our voice into a pale imitation of itself and leaves the rest to the imagination. We've lived with the phone medium for long enough that it doesn't seem artificial anymore. We'll go through the same acclimation process with our on-screen avatars. No doubt there will be something playful in exploring these new spaces with our virtual friends. But it won't be a game.

"*Namely, time spent watching television correlates with elevated body mass. Video game playing and other non-academic computer usage have been similarly indicted.*"

Video Gaming Increases the Risk of Obesity

Martin J. Atherton and James A. Metcalf

Martin J. Atherton and James A. Metcalf are contributors to American Journal of Health Studies. *The authors used surveys from the Center for Disease Control (CDC) as a means of determining the correlation between television, video games and elevated body mass index (BMI) in adolescents. According to their research, the relationship between video games and elevated BMI varied by gender.*

As you read, consider the following questions:

1. What are some of the obesity-related health issues that can occur?

Martin J. Atherton and James A. Metcalf, "Does Gender Modify the Impact of Video Game Playing and Television Watching on Adolescent Obesity?" *American Journal of Health Studies*, vol. 21, Winter/Spring, 2006, Copyright © 2006 American Journal of Health Studies. Reproduced by permission.

2. According to the article, which gender's body mass index (BMI) was more affected by video/computer game playing?

3. Which gender's weight seems to be more affected by television watching?

The objective of this study is to quantify the strength of association between selected behavioral and demographic factors and the risk of obesity among adolescents, respondents according to gender. Females reporting 5 or more hours of video/computer game playing were at significant risk for elevated BMI. Among males, significant risk ($p<0.05$) of elevated BMI was observed at 2 hours per typical school day and above. We controlled for both diet (intake) and exercise (expenditure) and still observed significant associations between elevated BMI and video game playing among females, and television watching among males.

Obesity Is a Health Crisis

Adolescent obesity and its health-related consequences have reached crisis proportions in the United States and drawn call to action from the Institute of Medicine. Moreover, obesity in children and adolescents lowers the age at which obesity-related health disorders occur, including cardiovascular disease, diabetes, hypertension, and depression. This disquiets epidemiologists and prompts them to identify potential risk factors for obesity.

Recent evidence has implicated both television watching and, to a less convincing extent, video-game playing and computer usage in adolescent obesity. Such associations are incompletely understood, but some consensus is emerging. Namely, time spent watching television correlates with elevated body mass. Video game playing and other non-academic computer usage have been similarly indicted.

Questions that remain unanswered include whether television watching and video/computer-game playing are markers of inactivity, markers of over-consumption, or of both? And, do these associations differ between males and females?

The purpose of this study is to measure the association between two sedentary behaviors, television watching and video/computer game playing, and elevated BMI according to gender.

The 2003 Youth Risk Behavior Survey (YRBS), which has been conducted by the Centers for Disease Control and Prevention (CDC) every other year since 1991, is the sample for this investigation. The YRBS is a multi-staged, weighted survey of health-related behaviors among American high school students. The overall response rate reported for 2003 is 67%. These data lie within the public domain and are available at www.cdc.gov/yrbs.

Behaviors Affect Adolescent Obesity

A total number of 14,106 respondents completed the YRBS survey and are included in this analysis. The mean age of female respondents is 16.2 years for non-elevated BMI and 16.1 years for elevated BMI. For males the mean age is 16.3 years for non-elevated BMI, and 16.3 years for elevated BMI.

We sought to determine the independent associations of two sedentary behaviors (television watching and video/computer game playing) with elevated body mass index while adjusting for demographic factors, daily exercise, and diet. Both unadjusted and adjusted odds ratios were obtained for all independent variables with respect to the dependent variable.

According to the Institute of Medicine, sedentary behavior is a leading risk factor for adolescent obesity. Two sedentary behaviors have been the focus of numerous studies: video/computer game playing and television watching. Their associations with elevated BMI appear to differ by gender.

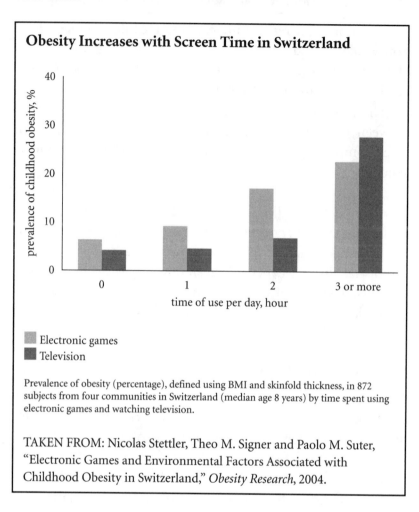

Obesity Increases with Screen Time in Switzerland

prevalence of childhood obesity, %

time of use per day, hour

Electronic games
Television

Prevalence of obesity (percentage), defined using BMI and skinfold thickness, in 872 subjects from four communities in Switzerland (median age 8 years) by time spent using electronic games and watching television.

TAKEN FROM: Nicolas Stettler, Theo M. Signer and Paolo M. Suter, "Electronic Games and Environmental Factors Associated with Childhood Obesity in Switzerland," *Obesity Research*, 2004.

For females, a significant increase in risk of elevated BMI was observed only at 5 or more hours per typical school day. For males, we observed no significant increases in risk of elevated BMI and hours of video/computer game playing.

We observed no increased risk of elevated BMI and hours spent watching television among females. By contrast, we observed significant increases in risk of elevated BMI among males at 2, 3, 4, and 5 or more hours of television watching on an average school day. For males, the adjusted odds ratios appear to increase linearly with increasing hours of television watching.

Thus, in adolescent obesity, video/computer game playing is a significant risk for females, but not males. Television watching is a significant risk for males, but not for females. Anti-obesity interventions might be more effective if gender differences are accommodated.

We observed increased risk for elevated BMI for both males and females who reported infrequent vigorous exercise of 20 or more minutes of duration. One might expect protective dietary effects on BMI since survey questions focused on consumption of healthful foods (fruits, vegetables, juices, and milk), but the pattern was mixed. For example, in males, eating no carrots appears to reduce risk, but so does eating carrots twice a day. Regardless, BMI is a reflection of caloric intake (diet) and metabolic expenditure (exercise). We controlled for exercise and patterns of food choice, not caloric consumption per se. We assumed that if patterns of food choice are similar, total caloric intake will also be similar.

Consistent with previous research (Atherton, 2005), we observed that the risk of elevated BMI varies by ethnic group. We also found that a rural domiciliary is protective among females but not males.

Caution is warranted when using self-reported data for weight and height. When, as in this survey, subjects are asked to recall exercise and dietary factors for the seven days preceding the survey, even more caution is indicated.

BMI is fundamentally a function of caloric intake and metabolic expenditure. Video game playing and television watching are associated with elevated BMI either as markers of increased caloric intake or of decreased metabolic expenditure. We controlled for both diet (intake) and exercise (expenditure) and still observed significant associations between elevated BMI and video/computer gaming playing among females, and television watching among males. The mechanisms underlying these gender-specific statistical associations remain unclear.

> *"All students can benefit from the unique qualities that these [video] games embody: adaptability, individualization, collaboration, experimentation, and role-playing as professionals."*

Video Games Can Enhance Sports Performance and Motivation

Elisabeth Hayes and Lauren Silberman

In the following viewpoint, the authors support the use of video games to enhance students' motivation, understanding, and performance in sports. They outline some characteristics of commercial off-the-shelf (COTS) games to support their points. They state that video games help students learn tactics and strategies, provide a safe environment, increase motivation, encourage teamwork, and enhance technical proficiency. Instructive features of games are also highlighted. Elisabeth Hayes is a professor and Lauren Silberman is a research scholar in the Department of Curriculum and Instruction at the University of Wisconsin in Madison.

Elisabeth Hayes and Lauren Silberman, "Incorporating Video Games into Physical Education," *JOPERD—The Journal of Physical Education, Recreation & Dance*, vol. 78, March 2007, pp. 18–24. Copyright © 2007 American Alliance for Health, Physical Education, Recreation and Dance. Reproduced by permission.

As you read, consider the following questions:

1. How do the authors say video gaming helps students who are less adept at sports and physical activities than their peers?

2. According to the authors, how does playing video games increase motivation to play sports?

3. How do young people make video gaming into a communal activity, rather than a solitary one, according to the authors?

Current cognitive theory supports the notion that the mind works by storing records of actual experiences and constructing intricate connections among them. From this perspective, human understanding consists of how people imagine, or simulate an experience in a way that prepares them for the actions they need and want to take in order to accomplish their goals. This notion of understanding is implicit in the use of mental-skills training in athletics, which engages athletes in creating mental images of successful performance. By engaging players in goal-directed actions within compelling virtual environments, video gaming can help players develop these mental models, or simulations of experience, in a more concrete and embodied sense than through mental imagery alone. Video gaming allows players to experience immediate and often unpredictable consequences from their actions. Since video games can portray a diverse range of potential situations, players can develop a much wider set of mental models of what to do, enabling them to make better and faster decisions during actual physical activities. . . . Visual simulation is effective for motor learning when the learner is intentionally using the simulation for learning and attempts to sense the execution of the simulated action by "getting into the body of the virtual player," [according to Yves-Andre Fery and Sylvain Ponserre].

Video Games Can Teach Strategy

While the above point refers broadly to how video gaming can develop an embodied understanding of physical performance, video games can also be used to help students acquire more specific declarative knowledge of strategies and tactics in sports and other physical activities. This is perhaps the most common reason that professional athletes use video gaming: to enhance their mastery of new strategies and to become more aware of and responsive to the strategies that might be used by their competitors. Video clips are already used by coaches and physical education instructors as tools for analyzing athletic performance. Video games offer the advantage of more closely tying observation and analysis to practice; a clip can be observed and then practiced immediately in the game, or a game play can be recorded and then observed and practiced once again. As Fery and Ponserre point out, sport video games provide very sophisticated virtual sequences in which learners can acquire appropriate knowledge. They offer examples from golf video games, which "provide bird's eye views together with virtual trajectories to explain the best approach to the hole or the most suitable alignment from a range of optional visual alignments between the club, the ball and the hole."

The realism of certain aspects of particular games can be used to introduce some key movement concepts. For example, in *Mario Power Tennis*, the power of a shot is affected by the (virtual) player's position relative to the ball, the ball's height, and the direction in which the player is headed when he or she strikes the ball. Since the video game user controls the virtual player's movements, the user may obtain feedback on the power required by viewing previously performed shots.

An important aspect of developing proficiency in a sport or other physical activity is learning its language (i.e., learning key terminology as a means of understanding the activity and communicating that understanding to others). Video games typically provide "situated" language learning, by integrating terminology into game play. For example, the names of particular moves may appear on the screen while they are executed, terminology may be reinforced orally as well as in writing, and in-game tutorials and game manuals often provide definitions and examples of movement language. In addition, games typically immerse players in simulated social worlds associated with sports, and players are often exposed to conversations and comments by virtual players who speak the language of that particular sport culture.

Practice in a Safe Environment

Video gaming, when done independently, offers a "sandbox," or psychological moratorium, where students can experiment with fewer risks to their self-esteem and physical safety. Mimicking a better player is a key to learning new athletic skills, and games offer ample opportunities for students to observe virtual players successfully execute skills that may be new to them. Students who are less adept than their peers can become familiar with various moves before engaging in the actual activity. Even more-experienced players may benefit from opportunities to observe and rehearse new skills in a low-threat environment. Students can also learn about team roles on their own before practicing these roles with their peers. By reducing the negative consequences of failure, video games can enhance students' self-image as athletes and increase the likelihood that they will experiment with new movements on the real athletic field.

Shelley Paul Smith persuasively argues for a broad view of differentiated instruction in physical education, across motor, cognitive, social, and affective domains of skill and knowledge. Video games offer considerable potential for tailoring the level of instruction to individual or group levels of proficiency in these domains. Many games can be played at various difficulty levels, and students can practice repeatedly until they achieve mastery. Even team sports can be practiced by individuals at their own level of performance. Video games might be effectively used for one or more learning stations, which allow students to practice different sets of skills in small groups.

Increased Motivation

The potential of video games to motivate engagement in prolonged and difficult learning is widely touted. This enhanced motivation is due, at least in part, to the opportunities that games afford players to take on and play with new and compelling identities. Players can imagine themselves as a favorite sports icon, a significant motivator given that, according to one study, 63 percent of 11- to 12-year-olds dream about being a sports star. Players can also create their own identity as an athlete. For example, *Madden* and *NCAA Football* allow gamers to create their own virtual players by designing body shape and skills, and to write their own name on the player's jersey. Games such as *Tony Hawk ProSkater* and Play[station] 2's *Home Run* give gamers the option of inserting their own photo as the face of their virtual player. In addition, students may be motivated by having a (virtual) professional athlete as an instructor, such as in the *Tiger Woods Golf* tutorial, where Tiger teaches players special shots. Success in a virtual sport can motivate students who otherwise would be reluctant to try out a new physical activity on their own. Anecdotal evidence suggests that some children who play sports games, such as basketball or tennis, become more motivated to participate in such sports. Furthermore, many young people who already have positive associations with video gaming may be motivated simply by the opportunity to "play" rather than "learn."

Various types of social interaction are obviously crucial in physical education, not only for the development of teamwork skills, but also for the creation of shared understandings of good practice. While many adults still hold an image of video gaming as a solitary pursuit, for young people such gaming is more often a communal activity. Games typically are designed to encourage competitive play, either face-to-face or online. Young people often watch each other play, alternate watching and playing, and engage in continuous conversation about game play. Online affinity groups associated with various games share information and strategies, and serve as a nexus for joint game play. These groups, which typically interact through fan sites on the Internet, can be tapped into as additional resources for learning and collaboration.

Video gaming can be used to enhance students' proficiency in using technology to support physical activity. This would help students meet two of the standards set by the International Society for Technology in Education: standard three (ability to use technology productivity tools) and standard six (ability to use technology problem-solving and decision-making tools). In addition, video gaming can be used as a starting point for students' use of the Web to locate information from fan sites, post advice and strategies, and discuss issues with a wide network of other players. Students can even learn about the use of design tools in games that offer user-creation options, such as *Tony Hawk Underground*'s design-a-skate-park or design-a-trick modes. . . .

Game Features Can Be Opportunities to Learn

Many games offer tutorials or embedded instruction to introduce new skills and scaffold the experience of new players. These tutorials are often quite sophisticated. For example, *World Soccer Winning Eleven 8 International* has four training options: beginner, free, situation, and challenge training. Beginner training teaches new players how to perform all the basic moves and explains the sport itself, the roles of the different players on the pitch, and even the offside rule (via a series of texts, diagrams, and demonstrations). Free training lets

---

A Selective List of Sports Video Games

Nearly all of these games release new editions every year. They are usually updated with new players and features. Typically, the newest games will be the best games to use. The games listed here are appropriate for most age levels. They play on consoles—such as PlayStation 2 [PS2], Xbox, or Game Cube [GC]—that link to a television. Many of these games are available for use on PCs [personal computers]. They range in price from $10 to $50, and consoles cost from $90 to $140.

Baseball
MLB Baseball PS2
MVP Baseball GC, PS2, Xbox, PC
Basketball
ESPN NBA 2k5 GC, PS2, Xbox
NBA Live GC, PS2, Xbox, PC
NBA Street GC, PS2, Xbox
Football
Madden NFL GC, PS2, Xbox, PC
NCAA Football GC, PS2, Xbox
Golf
Hot Shots Golf Fore! PS2
Tiger Woods PGA Tour PS2, Xbox, PC
Hockey
Gretzky NHL PS2
NHL Hockey GC, PS2, Xbox, PC

Soccer
FIFA Soccer GC, PS2, Xbox, PC
World Soccer Winning 8 Eleven International PS2, Xbox, PC
World Tour Soccer PS2
Tennis
Mario Power Tennis GC
WTA Tour Tennis GC, PS2
Other
Athens 2004 (Olympic game events) PS2
Dance Dance Revolution (Exergame-player moves on a dance pad to a song and movement sequence on screen) GC, PS2, Xbox
Rapala Pro Fishing PS2, Xbox, PC
Rugby 2005 PS2, Xbox
SSX (snowboarding) GC, PS2, Xbox
Summer Heat Beach Volleyball PS2
Tony Hawk Underground Series (skateboarding) GC, PS2, Xbox, PC

TAKEN FROM: Elisabeth Hayes and Lauren Silberman, "Incorporating Video Games into Physical Education," *JOPERD—The Journal of Physical Education Recreation and Dance*, March 2007.

---

players take control of a team on a field where the only opponent is a goalkeeper. Situation training teaches players how to use some of the more advanced controls to make them more effective at dribbling, passing, shooting, attacking, and defending. Challenge training is a series of increasingly difficult trials that test players' skills in eight different disciplines: attacking, defending, dribbling, short passing, manual passing, free-kick long passing, free-kick shooting, and ball possession.

As another example, the street basketball game, *NBA Street Volume 2* has a game mode called "Street School." In Street School, a coach, Stretch, guides players through 36 practice lessons divided into three categories: offense, defense, and advanced.

In many games, instruction is embedded in actual game play. For example, *Tony Hawk Underground*'s story mode introduces players to basic skateboarding moves through a series of challenges that advance the storyline, such as beating your best friend's score in a series of tricks.

Most COTS [commercial off-the-shelf] games come with brief written guides that include basic information such as how to use the game controller. Much more extensive information is usually available online, in formats ranging from player-created guides, FAQs [frequently asked questions], discussion boards, and walk-throughs, to more official manuals. These sites often sponsor online competitions and contests for related activities (e.g., best screen shot, best player-constructed skatepark). Players can also post "cheats" that can be useful in modifying the game parameters (and not necessarily to make the game easier).

These sites can also be used to help students gain information about the history of a sport and its prominent players and events. *NBA Street Volume 2*'s official Web site (http://www.easportsbig.com/games/nbastreet2/home.jsp#) has extensive information on the legendary players who appear in the game. Many games have such information embedded in the game. For example, a series of COTS games based on the Olympics (*Salt Lake City*, *Athens 2004* and *Visa Championships Torino 2006 Online Video Game*) allow players to experience

Olympic events such as archery, weightlifting, equestrian, track and field, swimming, and shooting. They can help students become familiar with various events, including real world records and times in real Olympic scenarios.

Commercial off-the-shelf games generally offer one or more of the following options for game play: (1) a single gamer controls a single virtual athlete, (2) multiple gamers each control a single virtual athlete, (3) a single gamer controls a virtual team, and (4) multiple gamers each control a virtual team. Each option offers somewhat different opportunities for learning. For example, the first mode allows students to become familiar with one sport or position on a team without the participation of other students or even a teacher. The second mode can be used to help students learn to collaborate with each other or even with a virtual partner. For example, in *Mario Power Tennis* a student can play doubles with three other classmates. The game can also provide a virtual athlete to fill in if one of the foursome is unavailable for practice.

In the third mode, a student can take on the role of coach, choosing the overall team strategy and monitoring the actions of all team members. Games such as *FIFA Soccer 2006* and *NHL Hockey* allow gamers to choose their team based on information such as player statistics. Most team-based options allow gamers to control a select number of team members. In *NBA Street*, players not only have to see the whole court and make play decisions, they must control all five team members on offense and defense simultaneously. By playing in these modes, students can begin to get a wider perspective on how a team functions, various player roles, and the importance of a unified team strategy. Team modes allow students to play different positions and experience a sport from various perspectives, leading to a better understanding of team sports as interconnected systems.

Parameters Are Customizable for Each Learner

In addition to player-configuration options, most COTS games are designed to accommodate different gamer ability levels and goals and to change the constraints of a particular setting. Many games can be played at different levels of difficulty, increasing the likelihood that all students can find a level that is challenging, yet not excessively frustrating. A number of games offer format options from mini-games to more extended "seasons," which can be selected according to the gaming time available in class or after school, or according to the goals of a particular unit or lesson. In some cases, games offer optional settings to increase the realism of game play. For example, *NHL Hockey* has an "action view" option that simulates the feeling of actually being on the ice, as opposed to a more aerial view. Many games offer location options, allowing the students or teacher to make choices about the particular stadium, golf course, skatepark, or other game conditions. These options can enhance student motivation by offering variety and by encouraging them to vary strategies to meet the demands of different contexts. As noted above, many games allow user creation of virtual athletes with different sets of strengths and limitations. This feature can be used to help students learn about the importance of acquiring various skills for success in different moves and strategies.

Commercial off-the-shelf games often include features intended to support post-game or even during-game analysis of moves and strategies. These features are valuable educational tools because they get students in the habit of thinking critically about game play. For example, *Tiger Woods PGA Tour 2004* offers a "mouse-motion swing," in which the tempo and pace of the player's entire backward and forward movement affect the final result. The point at which the player stops the mouse, the length of the movement, and the amount of side-to-side deviation affect the result as well. After the shot, the game delivers a painstaking analysis of each factor of the swing, thus allowing the player to work on perfecting the speed of his or her backswing, general tempo, and/or side-to-side variances. As another example, *Tony Hawk Underground 2* has "focus/slow-motion" control options, which allow players to see their moves displayed in slow motion while they are executing them. Many games allow the replay of game segments for post-game analysis. . . .

Educators Should Use Video Games in Physical Education

If educators accept the argument that COTS games have the potential to enhance physical play, then they should be willing to tap into this potential and experiment with new strategies for incorporating them into their gyms and classrooms. Children are more likely to be inactive and overweight now than ever before. So if they are not motivated by traditional methods of teaching sports and physical education, then conceivably it is time to find ways to employ a medium that many young people are familiar with and already enjoy.

Video games, when introduced into traditional classrooms, have been received with enthusiasm by students who are otherwise unexcited by the standard curricula. Likewise, video games may attract youths who are not typically interested in gym class and offer an alternative transition into sports and physical activity. All students can benefit from the unique qualities that these games embody: adaptability, individualization, collaboration, experimentation, and role-playing as professionals. Educators may find that video games are a stimulating and valuable addition to their instructional endeavors.

Periodical Bibliography

The following articles have been selected to supplement the diverse views presented in this chapter.

Mikael Blaisdell   "All the Right MUVEs: The Use of Computer Simulations That Appeal to Students' Love of Video Games Has Shown Compelling Educational Benefits," *THE Journal (Technological Horizons in Education)*, September 2006.

Preeta M. Banerjee   "Video Games Aren't a Waste of Time," *Business Week Online*, February 20, 2008.

Hope M. Cummings and Elizabeth A. Vandewater   "Relation of Adolescent Video Game Play to Time Spent in Other Activities," *Archives of Pediatric and Adolescent Medicine*, July 2007.

James Paul Gee   "High Score Education: Games, Not School, Are Teaching Kids to Think," *Wired*, May 2003.

Harvard Review of Health News   "How Video Games Affect Time Use," July 10, 2007.

Meryl Davids Landau   "Nine Reasons to Let Your Kids Play Video Games," *Redbook*, July 2006.

Aaron Levin   "Video Games, Not TV, Linked to Obesity in Kids," *Center for the Advancement of Health*, March 17, 2004.

Katherine Noyes   "Docs Retreat from 'Video Game Addiction' Diagnosis," *TechNewsWorld*, June 25, 2007.

Charlene O'Hanlon   "Eat Breakfast, Drink Milk, Play Xbox: The Daily Recipe for Students' Health and Fitness Is Taking on a New Ingredient Long Thought to Be a Poison: Video Games," *THE Journal (Technological Horizons in Education)*, April 2007.

Giles Whittell   "I Like Wind, Rain, Tents, Mountains, Fresh Air. That's Why My Children Won't Get Nintendos," *Times Online*, April 2, 2008.

CHAPTER 2

How Do Video Games Affect Society?

Chapter Preface

The *Tomb Raider* series of games, first released in 1996, has become so popular that it has spawned comic books, novels, theme park rides, and movies. The series' main character, British archaeologist and adventurer Lara Croft, has become a pop culture icon. As one of the few female protagonists in the video game world, Lara Croft has received both praise and criticism. Her character is tough, independent, and adventurous, and her creators earned kudos for presenting a strong and intelligent female character. The games have also drawn criticism for being sexist and demeaning, however, with many observers pointing out that Croft's large breasts are her most prominent physical feature.

The conventional wisdom is that most game players are teenage boys and young men, and many games are designed to gratify their tastes. Female gamers are often perceived as only playing "casual" games such as puzzle games, word games, and card games. The women and girls that do play more complex games such as *Tomb Raider* are divided in their opinions about the way women are depicted in video games or their absence from the games altogether. Some see the Lara Croft character as a heroic role model; others see her as degrading. Some think that many game characters can be seen as androgynous; others complain that more strong (but non-sexualized) female characters should be created.

Disagreement also exists about whether video games promote racial stereotypes. Some critics have asserted, for example, that African American men are too often portrayed as criminals. Others point out that in many games, players create their own characters, allowing them to be any race, color, or gender, often including a wide variety of possibilities that many people do not encounter in their real lives. They suggest that this variety of characters helps to break down stereotypical barriers.

The viewpoints in this chapter examine the relationship between video games and society. They discuss issues of gender, race, bigotry, and social tolerance. They also touch on the moral aspects of video games, considering whether they are injurious or beneficial to morality.

> "Games [such as Grand Theft Auto III]
> reduce America's ghettos and the bodies
> of color who inhabit these locales to
> spaces of danger and decay that neces-
> sitate state surveillance and regulation."

Video Games Promote Racism

David Leonard

*In the following viewpoint, David Leonard contends that al-
though much public debate about violence in video games exists,
racism has largely been ignored. He examines some of the legislative and popular critiques of video games, concluding that they
portray blackness as a source of moral indecency and cultural
decay. He also looks at the games themselves, particularly the
Grand Theft Auto series, pointing out elements he sees as racist
and arguing that games like these perpetuate racism and social
injustice. Leonard is an associate professor in the Department of
Comparative Ethnic Studies at Washington State University.*

As you read, consider the following questions:

1. What does Leonard say about the trend toward governmental regulation of video game content?

2. With the scene where the character Carl Johnson breaks into a house in *Grand Theft Auto: San Andreas*, how does the author describe the game's vision of the ghetto?

3. Why does the author say that the ghettocentric virtual reality of the *Grand Theft Auto* series matters?

While video games grew in popularity for several years, the release of *Grand Theft Auto III* (*GTA3*) in 2001 propelled the industry to new heights, resulting in several copycat games, including the game sequels *Grand Theft Auto: Vice City* (*GTA:VC*) and *Grand Theft Auto: San Andreas* (*GTA:SA*). While much has been made of the violent and sexual nature of this series, there has been little public debate or outcry regarding the racialized content of these games. Instead of condemning their promotion of stereotypes and the promotion of racialized state violence, which compared to the inclusion of sex and violence garners have no power in determining levels of participation, the likes of Hillary Clinton and David Walsh have denounced the series as a moral pollutant necessitating governmental action. It is in this context that this chapter explores the societal reaction to both *Grand Theft Auto III* and *Grand Theft Auto: San Andreas*, in terms of both political discourses and those of gamers. By examining online discussion groups, fan commentary, and political speeches (including those from elected and unelected "leaders") this [viewpoint] seeks to generate thoughts about the racial context of these games, generating insight as to how race contributes to both the societal condemnation and widespread popularity of these games and the racialized bodies that inhabit these virtual ghetto spaces.

Focusing on the racial content of these discourses, this [viewpoint] additionally makes note of the ways in which new racism defines yet simultaneously emanates from this discursive field. While offering some discussion of the ways in which these games deploy longstanding racialized stereotypes, how they offer primarily white suburbanites the opportunity to experience America's dangerous ghettos, and how they sanction and legitimize state violence, our focus here lends itself to the reactions—outrage and pleasure—of both cultural pundits/politicians and gamers, of both those who decry these games as a dangerous threat to children and those who celebrate these offerings of virtual reality as transgressive and even potentially oppositional, in the end demonstrating the centrality of race and violence within both discursive fields.

[Rapper] Dr. Dre once stated that "People in the suburbs, they can't go to the ghetto, so they like to hear what's goin' on. Everyone wants to be down." bell hooks, in *Outlaw Culture*, complicates this idea, situating processes of commodification, fetish and the pimping of a corporate ghettocentric imagination, arguing that "the desire to be 'down' has promoted a conservative appropriation of specific aspects of underclass black life, who in reality is dehumanized via a process of commodification wherein no correlation is made between mainstream hedonistic consumerism and the reproduction of a social system that perpetuates and maintains an underclass." Using such arguments of the basis of inquiry into the *Grand Theft Auto* series (most specifically *GTA:SA*), this [viewpoint] explores the ways in which the reaction, where race is explicitly absent yet central, legitimizes a conservative project that maintains a permanent underclass, whether in gamers' Internet discussions about the games, political rhetoric condemning the message of the game, or the consumptive pleasure derived from a ghetto existence that rarely penetrates American consciousness.

Calls for Legislative Regulation of Video Games

The release of *GTA:SA* in fall 2004 not only promoted lengthy wait-lists at Amazon.com, release parties throughout the nation, and ample online discussions, but [also] an infrequent level of unity in Washington, D.C. and in state capitals throughout the United States. During the subsequent six months, the calls for governmental intervention and legislative regulation over the content available within virtual gaming grew louder, especially after reports of the "hot coffee modification," which allowed players to simulate sex with naked women during *GTA:SA* play. In introducing the Family Entertainment Protection Act, Hillary Clinton called upon the government "to make sure their kids can't walk into a store and buy a video game that has graphic, violent, and pornographic content." Joseph Liebermann concurred, emphasizing the importance of protecting children from "a silent epidemic of media desensitification" and "for stealing the innocence of our children," pointing to the dangers of violent and overly sexualized games:

> There is a growing body of evidence that points to a link between violent video games and aggressive behavior in children. We are not interested in censoring video games meant for adult entertainment but we do want to ensure that these video games are not purchased by minors. Our bill will help accomplish this by imposing on those retailers that sell M-rated games to minors.

The Clinton and Liebermann legislation, which would prohibit the sale of "mature" games to anyone under the age of eighteen; order the FCC [Federal Communications Commission] to investigate "misleading" ratings and solicit complaints about video games; and require "an annual independent analysis of game ratings," along with their successful call for an investigation into *Rockstar* and *Grand Theft Auto* as a result of "hot coffee" controversy, demonstrates the level of interest and outrage emanating from political circles concerning portions of the virtual gaming industry. Ted Stevens, during hearings concerning the "decency" of computer games and television, captured the level of panic-driven anger directed at *GTA:SA* and the entire industry, all of which centers the notion of protecting America's youth (read: white middle class) from these indecent and immoral games: "America lacks the kind of moral compass the country should have for our young people." In his estimation and that of Clinton, Liebermann, and a host of others from both sides of the aisle, the government had to be that compass.

Such rhetoric and the calls for legislation are neither isolated nor particular to discourses emanating from Washington, D.C. From speeches on state House floors, to ample press releases, the condemnation of video games has become commonplace in recent years, as evident by the ubiquitous condemnation of *GTA:SA*. Following its release, Representative Fred Morgan, reflecting the nature of the discourse and the almost obsessive focus on video games as a cultural and moral pollutant, offered the following assessment of virtual gaming in a press release that called for legislation banning particular types of games within his state:

> If someone on the street offered to teach your children to decapitate their enemies, physically abuse women, and assassinate world leaders, you would probably call the police. But when a video game manufacturer provides the same "service," many parents are actually paying for their children to get a tutorial in violence and depravity. And instead of calling the police for help in many popular games your kids will be killing police.

Such outrage, rhetoric, and panics have promoted efforts to regulate video games in state after state, from Illinois and California to Michigan and Pennsylvania. In Illinois, Governor [Rod] Blagojevich led the first and most successful effort to regulate virtual reality. In fact, Governor Rod Blagojevich was the first public official to call for legislation that would make it illegal for anyone under the age of eighteen to buy violent or sexually explicit games: "This is all about protecting our children until they are old enough to protect themselves," the Governor stated in an issued statement. "There's a reason why we don't let kids smoke or drink alcohol or drive a car until they reach a certain age and level of maturity."

Fears of Ghettocentric Video Games

The trend toward governmental regulation of video game content, which has resulted in the courts overturning legislations that either restrict or seek to censor content, reflects a panic driven by a racial logic that fears the ghettocentric imagination available within contemporary gaming. The panics concerning the effects of (ghettocentric) video games on American (white middle-class) youth has not been limited to political officials seeking reelection and news coverage during relatively quiet times, but has found great resonance within church-based and otherwise conservative media organizations. The National Institute on Media and the Family (NIMF), led by Dr. David Walsh, has emerged as one of the most prominent critical voices directed at the video game industry. Providing "resources," reviews, and other information regarding the "appropriateness" of particular games for children, while lobbying politicians and game retailers to protect "children and teens" from "killographic" and sexual content, NIMF embodies this ongoing culture war. Others, like The Lion and Lamb Project and Mothers Against Video Game Addiction and Violence (MAVAV), have been equally instrumental in successfully pushing the issue of the effects of video games within American culture and in turn defining the nature of the discourse. For example, MAVAV recently compared playing video games to alcohol and drug abuse, working toward "educating parents" on "today's fastest and increased threat and danger to our children's health and way of life."

What links together these various voices, as well as others (such as those panic-driven debates regarding the effects of video games found on numerous white nationalist Web sites) is not merely the reduction of video games to a pollutant on American cultural values, the threat that both sexually-explicit and violent games pose to youth, or the reconstitution of the state as institution that is supposed to protect children, but the types of games that cause outrage, induce panics, result in anxiety, and warrant governmental/communal intervention: those inside American ghettos and allowing players to "become gangstas." It was *GTA:SA*, not even *Grand Theft Auto III*, that lead to calls for legislation. This is not a coincident and reveals much about the nature of a discourse as it was a virtual world of street gangs, drive-by shootings, and strong-armed robberies that sent America's political, moral, and cultural elites into a tizzy. While reflective of a myriad of factors, it is not surprising that *GTA3*, with its celebration of an Italian mob family and racial tropes, never resulted in national debates and cries for governmental intervention.

In the end, it was the release of *50 Cent: Bulletproof, The Warriors, 187: Ride or Die, Narc,* and *True Crime: Streets of LA/NY,* as well as the proposed release of *25 to Life* and *Gang Wars,* and not *America's Army, Socom,* or any number of war games that encourage youth to kill, destroy and maim that prompted calls for protection. It is not truly about violence, or even the effects of violence on youth, but their exposure to particular types of violence, with violence committed by gangsters and criminals, particularly those of color, who also seem to represent a disproportionate number of these characters, against the state identified as a significant threat against the moral and cultural fabric of the nation. Violence committed by the state, whether from a virtual military or police force, which tend to be overwhelmingly white within virtual reality, is certainly not a threat or dangerous to America's youth; in fact, it seems as if the discourse constructs these type of games as offering a desirable message concerning safety, security and the state, as needed to control the savages who inhabit the Third World or America's inner cities. While ignoring the racial aspects of this process, Clive Thompson describes the outrage directed toward video games as being based in the celebration of state violence as opposed to individual violence or criminality as the basis of which games receive praise and which elicit cultural panics:

> Nine times out of 10, when you're blowing people's chests open with hollow-point bullets, you aren't playing as a terrorist or criminal. No, you're playing as a cop, a soldier or a special-forces agent—a member of society's forces of law and order. . . . Yet anti-gaming critics didn't really explode with indignation until *Grand Theft Auto III* came along. . . . Why weren't these detractors equally up in arms about, say, the *Rainbow Six* series? Because games lay bare the conservative logic that governs brutal acts. Violence—even horrible, war-crimes-level stuff—is perfectly fine as long as you commit it under the aegis of the state. If you're fighting creepy Arabs and urban criminals, go ahead—dual-wield those Uzis, equip your frag grenades and let fly. Nobody will get much upset.

Although Thompson offers a powerful assessment of the current discourse concerning video games, he fails to consider the racial implications here, with a vast majority of current outrage being directed toward ghetto or hip-hop (those defined by blackness) games. The Family Media Guide top 10 most violent games for 2005 includes six games which all offer gang narratives concerning inner city crime. The supposed lack of values in "those communities" reflects the focus on protecting children from ghetto violence in ways beyond formal segregation. In this scenario, inner-city kids are already lost due to their daily exposure to violence and a "culture of poverty." This discourse ultimately reifies commonsense understandings of blackness as a source of moral indecency and cultural decay. To understand the efforts of Clinton, Lieberman or Walsh is to move beyond a focus on generational splits, geographic battles, or mere cultural/value differences. More importantly, as evidenced by varied reactions to the various installments of *GTA* series, the publicity afforded to the "hot coffee modification" controversy, or the questions, if not panics, afforded to the release of a wave of ghettocentric video games, demonstrates the racial nature of panics, that public displays of blackness, that the presumed opportunity to "become" a black thug or visit America's ghettos, fulfill longstanding fears of black sexuality, physicality, and violence, contributing to a particularly powerful panic centering on the effects of virtual blackness on white suburban youth. The series of moral panics that constructed these virtual ghettocentric spectacles as transgressive, as violations of community standards, rather than commodities that not only sought to capitalize on the publicity resulting from such panics, reflects a longstanding white supremacist fears about black masculinity, sexuality, and violence. . . .

Racial Characteristics of *Grand Theft Auto*

Amid the widespread debates about the *GTA* series, and particularly *GTA:SA*, as to its effects on children, and the impact of playing highly sexualized and violent games, little has been made of the racial content, particularly how these games reinforce dominant understandings of America's ghettos, blackness, and state control. As with the discussion, these games reduce America's ghettos and the bodies of color who inhabit these locales to spaces of danger and decay that necessitate state surveillance and regulation. Although the panics and celebration routinely come from outside of urban communities of color, a sustained engagement from within communities of color and other anti-racist advocates is necessary given the ways in which these games legitimize dominant racial discourses and practices. A defining characteristic of *Grand Theft Auto: San Andreas* is the ability to commit home invasion robberies, on top of the usual murders, pimping, car theft and other missions. Carl Johnson—the player-controlled character—along with your crew can sneak into "innocent people's" homes in search of goods and cash to steal. At some points in

Video Games Stereotype Asians

After an eight-month study of [racism in video games, Robert] Parungao concluded that racist stereotypes, which draw condemnation in other forms of media such as television and film, are quite prevalent in games. A fifth-generation Canadian of Chinese and Filipino descent, Parungao focused his research on Asian stereotypes and took an in-depth look at *Grand Theft Auto III*, *Shadow Warrior*, *Warcraft 3*, and *Kung Fu*.

Parungao noted that nonwhite characters in *Grand Theft Auto III* were mainly criminals and obstacles to be disposed of by the white hero. He also focused on the lack of distinction between Asian cultures in *Shadow Warrior*.

"The villain in *Shadow Warrior* goes by a Chinese name, Lo Wang," Parungao said in a statement. "But when he fires his rocket launcher at his enemies, he screams 'just like Hiroshima.'"

Parungao said games aren't subjected to the same scrutiny from minority groups that other media endure. Consequently, the industry has not seen the same changes in minority portrayal that those media have.

Brendan Sinclair,
"Student Thesis Pegs Games as Racist,"
July 24, 2006. www.gamespot.com.

the game, home invasions allow you to sneak up on sleeping families, holding them at bay with a shotgun or another weapon of your choice. During one game playing session, Carl breaks into a house, only to find an unsuspecting white couple. As the white male resident attempts to protect his blonde wife by challenging Carl to a fight, he states: "you probably can't read." As with the rest of the game, this standoff, with Carl murdering these two individuals, further solidifies hegemonic visions of the ghetto as a war zone inhabited by black gangstas that not only prey on black residents, but those white families living outside its virtual ghetto center.

Another important element of *GTA:SA* is how this game disseminates dominant ideologies and common sense ideas of race toward the sanctioning of state violence. Beyond playing on hegemonic visions of people of color and criminality, *GTA:SA* equally deploys reactionary visions of communities of color through its narrative and virtual representations. For example, as you drive throughout and between the game's various cities, the radio not only blasts a spectrum of jams, all of which further reflects the commodification of an imagined urban black aesthetic, but a series of reactionary public service announcements, which embody a virtual moral panic and contribute to those efforts outside of this virtual urban space. Paired with the deployment of racialized images of criminality (even black cops are corrupt), dysfunctionality and danger, these radio spots highlight the game's reactionary political orientation, playing on hegemonic myths of race, class and nation. "Notice food lines are getting too long. Wonder why? 19 million illegal aliens are in this country. Most are in San Andreas." The violence and mayhem that define this virtual reality reflect the number of illegal aliens that view America as a place of handouts. Obviously playing on white supremacist mythology of immigration and welfare, such representations justify increased spending on the war against immigrants—decreasing the social welfare budget while increasing the power of the state to police borders would be productive in solving this problem. In another instance, the game reflects on the state of poverty and welfare inside this virtual America. "Those of you, who are poor, should just stop whining. Enjoy it and sit back to do what you do best: watch TV." In a third moment, a talk radio show further articulates the racist orientation of the game and its effort to link representation and state violence. Amid a talk show debate concerning immigration into San Andreas, one contributor noted how Asian immigrants were flooding the area with drugs while those from South America brought nothing since "South America has less culture than a toilet bowl." In each instance, the game gives voices to white supremacist ideologies legitimized by the game's narrative and racialized representation, sanctioning the current course of state violence. *GTA:SA* is not simply teaching kids to be violent, but eliciting consent for the ways the state enacts violence on communities of color.

Murder Discriminates and Faces Selective Consequences

While unable to provide a complete analysis of the ways in which the *GTA* series aid white supremacist discourses and practices, each of which has elided the dominant discourse, I think it is important to make mention of a key narrative element that further illustrates its sanctioning, if not promotion of state violence, that has a particular effect on communities of color. Whether participating in an urban colonial project of taking territory, or participating in random acts of virtual violence, a core element of *GTA:SA* is the murdering of people of color. While this premise is a defining character of this genre of games, *GTA:SA* elucidates the role (or lack thereof) of the state in protecting and serving communities of color. Throughout the game, the police ignore the murder of other "gang members," often intervening only in moments where violence is directed at the "innocent." In other words, Carl can, at times, kill rival gang members in front (or close to) police without consequences. Killing an innocent citizen brings the police swiftly and with the full force of the law. Furthermore, as these individuals lie in the street in virtual wait for medical attention, the paramedics rarely arrive. The murder of the innocent in the game frequently leads to not only a quick ambulance response, but also the resuscitation of these characters. *GTA:SA*, thus, concretizes hegemonic ideologies regarding criminality and the state's role in only protecting the "innocent." It reveals the nature of new racism, which celebrates the visibility and commodifiable opportunities available to people of color, even as those outside the cultural landscape and the representations within popular culture as subjected to regulation and demonization. . . .

Video Games Promote an Understanding of Blackness

The widespread debate between gamers (players, designers, industry supporters, academics) and the "haters" (politicians, media critics, conservative cultural groups, and the religious right) have successfully erased the racist, patriarchal, heteronormative, and xenophobic representational and textual utterances of the entire series. From its reification of blackness as the ontological sign of decay and moral indecency to its demonization of Latino immigrants as economic parasites, the manner in which these games uncritically give life and voice to "concrete practice and other banalities of national evil," is elided from the discourse. Likewise, the dialectics between the virtual and the real, whether in discourse (culture of poverty, the racialization of communities of color) and practice (police brutality; the war on drugs) is further obscured by the discursive focus on sex, violence, and the efforts to protect the purity and innocence of (some) children.

Notwithstanding the rhetoric of protecting children from harmful representations of black men, or the virtual erasure of women of color, none of these officials have publicly denounced or called for regulation of racist or racialized games. These same legislative bodies have not elucidated plans to insulate "our children" from white supremacist narratives promulgated by the video game industry. None have questioned the racial content of games like *Grand Theft Auto: San An-*

dreas. There is no discourse concerning the dissemination of racial stereotypes or the affirmation of the racist status quo. Outrage remains in a discourse of children, its focus being violence and sexual content, rather than the effects/significance of these games in society, especially as spaces of racial meaning and state violence. The nature of *Grand Theft Auto* reflects this fact, as does the silence of politicians, cultural commentators and antiracist proponents; make clear about war against youth.

While the motivations of profit and appealing to a marketplace driven by the allure of hip-hop and black cultural styles with white consumers drives the continued production of games like *GTA:SA* or *Gang Wars*, its gaming dimensions and its surrounding discourse of reception (celebration and condemnation) must be understood within a racial context. "The black other occupies a complex site, a place where fears, desires, and repressed dreams are lodged," argues Norman Denzin. More than fears and repressed dreams, the black body and those racialized spaces exist in virtual reality and the national imagination as "a site of spectacle, its blackness" existing as "a potential measure of evil, and menace," necessitating containment and control. The representation of blackness or inner-city communities through a hegemonic ghettocentric imagination, the celebrations of adults becoming gangstas, and the fears caused by the appearance of hypersexual and violent ghetto games follows longstanding white supremacist logic that "focuses, organizes, and translates blackness into commodifiable representations and desires that [can] be packaged and marketed across the landscape of American popular culture" or otherwise confines it outside the dominant racial order. In other words, black bodies will continue to be marketed and commodified by a global video game industry just as those same bodies will be subjected to the rules and logic that emanate from white supremacy.

Moreover, the similarity in frames and discursive logic that emanate from all circles (haters and players alike) reveals that its providing players the chance to don the costume (hair, muscles, tattoos, gear) of a true "gangsta" or visiting America's most violent spaces does not represent a transgression to traditional (white supremacist, hetero-normative, patriarchal) values that is either worthy of condemnation or celebration, illustrating how corporate commodification reifies dominant ideologies and racial/gender/sexual logics, all while the game industry cashes in on their ghettocentric representations, politicians and other public figures cash in on the controversy and moral panics, and gamers continue to cash in on their whiteness.

As politicians focus on video game violence and the moral offerings within gaming culture, thereby eluding the racial and ideological dimensions of these games and ignoring broader societal problems, and its defenders obscure similar dimensions and their connections to virtual reality, it is important to remember that the *GTA* series, *GTA:SA* particularly, and a ghettocentric virtual reality matters because racism kills—the celebrations and demonizations of blackness jointly facilitate the hegemony of new racism, which in the end maintains color lines and white privileges, whether manifesting in the perpetuation of the prison industrial complex or systemic poverty that reared its head in wake of Hurricane Katrina. It matters because social justice—the ability of all people to live their lives free of oppressions based on race, class, gender, sexuality, and ideology—is a goal that U.S. society has long forgone for profit at any cost. It has never been "just a game." It has always been lives, livelihoods, injustice, and a desire for much, much more.

> "Players can realize that there are many
> possible ways to deal with their per-
> sonal and social reality. Hopefully, this
> might lead to the development of a tol-
> erant attitude that accepts multiplicity
> as the rule and not the exception."

Video Games Can Teach Social Tolerance

Gonzalo Frasca

In this viewpoint, Gonzalo Frasca claims that video games can be used to deal with human relationships and social issues and to encourage critical thinking skills. Frasca compares interactive simulations in video games to narratives and traditional drama, which are more linear and fixed in nature. He discusses a theater technique that presents a problem to be solved and continues with improvisation that leads participants to a discussion of "what could happen." He contends that this model can be used with video games, citing The Sims *as a game that begins to involve gamers in critical development. Frasca is a game developer, researcher, and entrepreneur.*

As you read, consider the following questions:

1. According to Frasca, what is Augusto Boal's goal with the "Theater of the Oppressed"?

2. Briefly describe how the author explains that someone being bullied at school can use a *Pac-Man* template to illustrate his problem, and give at least one solution that might be offered by another player.

3. What kind of questions does the author say *The Sims* produces because it portrays people and not aliens?

Bertolt Brecht's [German playwright and director (1898–1956)] drama challenged Aristotle's ideas [of comedy and tragedy, in which plot—rather than characters—is most important]: . . . He argued that Aristotelian theater keeps the audience immersed without giving them a chance to take a step back and critically think about what is happening on the stage. Brecht created several techniques in order to alienate what is familiar in the play, constantly reminding the spectators that they were experiencing a representation and stimulating them to think about what they were watching. Brecht's techniques, however, were not exclusively targeted at the audience. He also encouraged performers to be completely aware of their actions. Instead of being "inside the skin" of the character, he encouraged having a critical distance that would let them understand their role.

The Theater of the Oppressed

Brazilian dramatist Augusto Boal took Brecht's ideas even further by creating a set of techniques, known as the "Theater of the Oppressed" (TO), that tear down the stage's "fourth wall." Boal's main goal is to foster critical thinking and break the actor/spectator dichotomy by creating the "spect-actor," a new category that integrates both by giving them active participation in the play. The repertoire of techniques of TO is ex-

tremely large and includes, among others, the "invisible theater"—where actors work "undercover" in public spaces—and
the "Forum Theater."

Forums are created around a short play (five to 10 minutes long), usually scripted on-site, and based on the sugges-
tions of the participants. The scene always enacts an oppres-
sive situation, where the protagonist has to deal with powerful
characters that do not let her achieve her goals. For example,
the play could be about a housewife whose husband forbids
her to go out with her friends. The scene is enacted without
showing a solution to the problem. After one representation,
anybody in the audience can take over the role of the protagonist and suggest, through her acting, a solution that she thinks
would break the oppression. Since the problems are complex,
the solutions are generally incomplete. This is why the process
is repeated several times, always offering a new perspective on
the subject. In Boal's own words: "It is more important to
achieve a good debate than a good solution." It is central to
stress that Boal uses theater as a tool, not as a goal per se. In
other words, the ultimate objective of Forum Theater plays is
not to produce beautiful or enjoyable performances, but rather
to promote critical discussions among the participants. Unlike
traditional theater that offers just one complete, closed sequence of actions, Forum Theater sessions show multiple perspectives on a particular problem. They do not show "what
happened" but rather "what could happen." It is a theater that
stresses the possibility of change, at both social and personal
levels.

For these reasons, TO is a perfect model for creating non-
Aristotelian, nonimmersive videogames. . . . While Boal certainly uses theater techniques, his work is closer to games and
simulation than to theater. As performance theorist Philip
Auslander argues, Boal had to give up performance altogether
in order to bridge the gap between performers and spectators.

Snapshots

Go! Go! Go! Go!

© Love A78

The hot new video game where you're a peacemaker
who disarms everyone in sight and sells them on
the virtues of nonviolent communication.

"The hot video game where you're a peacemaker who disarms everyone in sight and sells them on the virtues of nonviolent communication." Cartoon by Jason Love. www.Cartoonstock.com.

Forum Theater is nothing but a game, with specific rules, that uses theater to simulate certain events and behaviors. . . .

A Game Based on Boal's Forum Theater

The following technique is a computer-based equivalent of Boal's Forum Theater that uses videogame rather than drama. Instead of performing on a stage, participants would discuss real-life situations by creating videogames and then modifying them in order to reflect their personal points of view.

Forum Videogames could work as a feature available inside a bigger "Videogames of the Oppressed" online community. It would be targeted to a homogenous small group—for example, a class of high school teenagers—coordinated by a moderator. Any participant—who will be referred as the "protagonist"—would be able to start a forum. The protagonist would be able to design one or a series of videogames where she would try to simulate a problematic situation that she is trying to deal with. The process of videogame design would be done by modifying preexistent templates based on classic videogames (*Space Invaders, Street Fighter, Pac-Man,* etc).

Once the game is ready, the protagonist would post it online, allowing the rest of the group to play with it. Players would be able to post their written comments and even submit a modified version of the game that reflects their personal position towards the protagonist's problem. The modified version could be a variant of the protagonist's original game, or a brand new game based on a different template. The process would repeat many times, just as it happens in Forum Theater, triggering new designs and discussions.

For example, let's imagine that the protagonist's problem is that he is being bullied at school and he doesn't know how to deal with this. In order to simulate his problem, he could use a *Pac-Man* template and modify the original game. He would replace the Pac-Man with a cartoon version of himself and replace the ghosts with images of his harassers. In addition to this, he could also take away the score feature and the pills, leaving nothing but a labyrinth where he is being constantly chased. Once that game is posted online, the other members of the group could respond by creating variants. One of them could be to modify the structure of the labyrinth to create a small space where the protagonist could live isolated, safe from the bullies. But other players could say that this means giving up his freedom and, therefore, that it is not a good solution. Then, another player could suggest using violence, by introducing weapons on the environment. Another may suggest introducing more players (several Pac-Mans) who would stick together and defend themselves as a group of virtual vigilantes. Of course, somebody may argue that it is technically impossible to be all the time surrounded by your friends: the bullies will find you alone sooner or later.

Again, the goal of these games is not to find appropriate solutions, but rather serve to trigger discussions—which could take place in person or through online chat. It would not matter if the games could not simulate the situation with realistic accuracy. Instead, these games would work as metonyms that could guide discussions and serve to explore alternative ways of dealing with real life issues.

The Sims as a Simulation

The Sims represents a breakthrough in videogame design. For the first time, a best-selling game is not about trolls and wizards. This simulation is about regular people—known as Sims—in everyday situations in an American, suburban environment.

In my opinion, The Sims's biggest achievement was that it fully opened the Pandora's box of simulating human life. Although structurally The Sims is similar to other resource management simulations, the fact that it portrays people, and not aliens, results in players asking questions about the game's ideology. Is it okay to let a Sim starve to death? Is it possible to have same-sex Sims relationships? What about threesomes? Will I spoil my Sim child if I buy her too many toys? All these questions would have probably never been asked if the game had been about monsters or aliens. The fact that the best-selling game of the year 2000 was about people is a clear sign that videogames are on their way towards maturity.

For ages, our civilization has been learning to deal with the issues of representation, including concerns about its accuracy and its limits. Videogames like *The Sims* are introducing to the masses a different form of representation—simulation—which has always been present in our culture through games, but that now can dare to start modeling more complex systems, such as human life. Even if *The Sims* is a very limited model of human relationships, it is a harbinger of videogames as a mature communicational and artistic form.

The Sims's constraints are many. For example, Sims cannot communicate in a verbal language and their personal relationships are not described with depth. In addition, the consumerist ideology that drives the simulation is nothing short of disturbing: the amount of friends that you have literally depends on the number of goods that you own and the size of your house. Nevertheless, simulation is an extremely complex task and, despite its shortcomings, *The Sims* succeeds at delivering an enjoyable game involving human characters.

The game allows players to create their own skins and designs and then share them online. However, the designers did not create an open environment where players could modify the rules of the simulation by coding new behaviors and objects. This is understandable from a marketing perspective: software companies want both to retain authorial control over their productions and to prevent players from creating controversial materials.

What follows is a description of how a hypothetical, open-source, modified version of *The Sims* could serve as an environment for players to distance themselves from the representation and engage in critical discussions. My intention is to show that Boal's ideas could also be used in mainstream videogame design. Although my previous example was better suited for small groups, educational or therapeutic environments, this one could appeal to a larger community of players.

In traditional videogames, the player "is" the character. In *The Sims* the player can control the character in a less direct way. However, *The Sims*'s characters are generally flat, because most of their differences are based either on their moods, or on visual traits that do not affect their behavior. This would be solved if players had more control over character creation by deciding their behavioral rules instead of just selecting their clothes. In order to encourage critical debate, the modified version of *The Sims* that I propose would allow players to modify the internal rules of the characters. The basic gameplay would be similar to the current game but, in addition to downloadable objects and skins, it would also be possible to get user-designed characters with different personalities and particular sets of actions. These characters would be created with a special tool that would require programming. Players would be able to rate the different characters and even create their own versions, based on behavioral details that they think need improvement in order to attain a higher level of realism. Both behaviors and comments would be available online in a "Character Exchange" site.

A Sample Scenario

The following is a sample scenario of a particular session, based on the rules that I am proposing:

Agnes has been playing with the simulation for many days. She knows its basic dynamics and enjoys it. Nevertheless, she feels that it would be better if family relationships were more realistic. So, she goes to the "Character Exchange" Web site and browses through different characters. She finds one that looks interesting. It is called "Dave's Alcoholic Mother version 0.9," and it has the following description:

> This mother spends a lot of time working, and she is very tired when she gets back home. Still, every night she has to fix dinner and do some housecleaning. She can get very an-

noyed by children and pets and may become violent. In order to escape from her reality, she drinks a lot of bourbon.

Agnes considers giving it a try and downloads it into one of the houses with which she has been playing. Agnes's virtual household is composed of a couple, three children, and a cat. After the download, her original mother character is replaced by "Dave's Alcoholic Mother version 0.9." Agnes finds the character quite interesting. After playing with it for a while, she realizes that when the mother reaches a certain degree of fatigue, she starts drinking. The more she drinks, the less she will care about her family. She remains calm unless her husband insists on cuddling or giving her a back rub.

Although Agnes thinks that the character is pretty well-depicted, there are details that she does not agree with. For example, the character always gets her drinks from the little bar in the living room. Agnes knows from personal experience that, in general, alcoholics hide their bottles around the house and try not to drink in public. So, she goes back to the "Character Exchange" and writes a public critique of Dave's creation. After doing this, she tries alternative alcoholic-mother behaviors. If the available characters do not satisfy her, she can modify one of the available versions and introduce a new behavior that makes the mother hide her alcohol bottles. She can then post this new character online and make it available to other players.

Some weeks later, Agnes gets a little tired of playing with her character and wants to give her some more personality. So, she decides that it would be great if she could add some extra behavioral code to it. Agnes downloads a character described as "Peter's Radical Greenpeace Activist version 9.1." After some editing and modifications, Agnes introduces this behavior to her alcoholic-mother character. The new character would still be an alcoholic, but she would take more care of plants, recycle everything and would never kick her cat while drunk.

The Problems of Simulation Building

As I previously said, the biggest obstacle for building Boalian videogames lies in the fact that programming simulated behaviors is an extremely difficult and time-consuming task. Even with a design tool that involved templates or some kind of visual object-oriented programming, it is likely that the average player would consider the task overwhelming. Still, as Amy Bruckman's work on *MOOSE Crossing*—an object-oriented, multi-user dungeon where participants can modify the environment by creating new objects—suggests, players can become really involved with programming simulated features and will exchange tips and help with others who are less skilled programmers.

Although it is possible that certain players could deal with the programming of new behaviors, it is likely that most participants would only be able to download behaviors made by others. I think that even if most players would not be able to code their own features, they could at least tinker with preexisting behaviors. The fact that a single behavior such as alcoholism could be available in so many different versions from players from different social and cultural backgrounds would encourage players to think about issues such as social construction of reality—but also about defending their points of view and listening to alternative opinions.

Of course, the lack of programming proficiency is not the only problem that Boalian videogame designers would face. However, the popularity of simulators such as *The Sims* or *SimCity* may serve as a tool for transforming the perception of videogames from interactive narratives into simulated models. As the public becomes more familiar with manipulating and modifying simulations, the concept of designing their own may become more appealing.

Games to Help Raise Critical Awareness

The two examples that I just gave should be considered more as illustrations of the paths that could be taken in order to design Boalian videogames than as blueprints for actual systems. The main goal of these examples is to show that videogames could be used as tools for better understanding reality and raising critical awareness among players. Current Aristotelian videogame design paradigms such as immersion should not be taken for granted, since questioning the values and mechanics of videogames could also be a source of engagement for players.

The main problem with these examples is that they require players to be very good programmers, a prerequisite that might be impossible to attain. Nevertheless, there may be some possible solutions to this problem. Further details on these techniques can be found in "Videogames of the Oppressed," a thesis developed at the Georgia Institute of Technology and on which this article is based.

When I describe these ideas to fellow researchers or game designers, they usually ask me if I really believe that social and personal change is possible through videogames. My answer is always a straight "no." Neither art nor games can change reality, but I do believe that they can encourage people to question it and to envision possible changes.

Unlike narrative, simulations are a kaleidoscopic form of representation that can provide us with multiple and alternative points of view. By accepting this paradigm, players can realize that there are many possible ways to deal with their personal and social reality. Hopefully, this might lead to the development of a tolerant attitude that accepts multiplicity as the rule and not the exception.

| "It is often through games that boys and men become proficient with computer technology. The gender gap in computer-game play results in a gender gap in computer literacy."

More Computer Game Designs Should Appeal to Women

Elizabeth Sweedyk and Marianne de Laet

Elizabeth Sweedyk and Marianne de Laet are associate professors at Harvey Mudd College, and they teach a class on gender and computer games. In the following viewpoint, they assert that although many women play computer games, the games are usually puzzles or card games instead of what they call "real" games, which have three-dimensional worlds and intricate play. They compare games traditionally marketed to boys with those marketed to girls, concluding that new game designs that include female players are needed. They also describe some new games designed by their students.

Elizabeth Sweedyk and Marianne de Laet, "Women, Games, and Women's Games," *Phi Kappa Phi Forum*, Summer 2005, pp. 25–28. Copyright © 2005 Phi Kappa Phi Forum. Reproduced by permission.

As you read, consider the following questions:

1. What male stereotypes do the authors say most "real" games value?

2. Why do the authors say girls did not play "pink" games that were developed after *Barbie Fashion Designer?*

3. What characteristics do the authors say new kinds of games will have if gender is problematized instead of dichotomized?

During the last twenty years, computer and video games have become a huge commercial market. But as the computer-game industry has grown, it has spawned a gender gap—a gap that shows up in the demographics of computer-game players and designers alike. Games are, for the most part, built by and for men. And when the industry *does* target girls and women, it usually fails miserably.

We should care about this, for it is often through games that boys and men become proficient with computer technology. The gender gap in computer-game play results in a gender gap in computer literacy. Furthermore, computer games are a source of enormous pleasure for men; women are arguably missing out. Finally, computer games have become a powerful cultural force; as compelling, interactive, and immersive environments for storytelling, they have the potential to reshape perspectives, norms, and values. If such a reshaping is taking place, women need to have a voice in this process.

So why is it that women do not play computer games? Can we—should we—build games for women? If so, what would these games be like? And would women play them? To explore these questions—and the assumptions and values that we bring to them—we have developed a new course on gender and computer games that combines cultural criticism of games with game-building exercises. Our course mixes theory and practice—computer science and cultural analysis. With this course we aim to bring together men and women from a variety of disciplines and with different levels of expertise in the development of digital technology. We seek to provide budding game designers and builders with the tools of cultural criticism. Most importantly, we want to interest women in game-building—because we believe that their involvement will lead to better games.

Why Women Don't Play Computer Games

Common wisdom has it that women do not play computer games. Or do they? Actual numbers are much higher than one might guess: almost 40 percent of all computer/video-game players are female, and for online games the number is more than 50 percent. If these statistics surprise you, think *Bejeweled*, think *Solitaire*, think online *Bridge*. These are the games that women play; these are the games that they play a lot.

But *Bejeweled*, *Solitaire*, and *Bridge* do not spring to mind when we think "computer game." Our students—who are, after all, the experts on computer games—tell us that *Bejeweled*, *Solitaire*, and *Bridge* are not "real" computer games. Yes, these are games; yes, these games are played on computers—but real computer games they are not. What, then, makes a computer game "real"? Is it a matter of cost and revenue? Is it a matter of genre? Is it game play, or graphics, or technical complexity?

We know "real" games when we see them: *Grand Theft Auto, Halo, Half-Life*. These games offer rich, three-dimensional (3D) worlds, complex technology, and intricate game play. They are expensive and time-consuming. They are games that gamers play. But what matters is not so much what these games *are*, but what they *do*: these "real" games *make* gamers. They act as rites of passage into the gaming world. "Real" games are the material objects around which this gaming culture organizes; they are the objects by which the culture defines itself. These games embody the shifting and unarticulated aesthetic of the gaming community—and it is embracing this aesthetic that makes one a player in this community. But as the gaming culture defines "real" games it also defines what does not count as "real." The misperception that women do not play computer games stems from the fact that the gaming culture does not consider the games that they *do* play as "real."

Games for Boys and Men

Computer and video games have not always been toys for boys. In 1972, Magnavox marketed the first home console, the Odyssey, as a family-entertainment device. Early games such as *Pong* were gender neutral; they bear far less resemblance to present-day "real" games than they do to games such as *Bejeweled*. But the evolution of computer games went hand in hand with advancements in computer graphics. The power of computers to create fully interactive three-dimensional worlds was seized by technology developers to create worlds that realized their fantasies. These developers were men; their fantasies led to game formulas that are highly gendered.

Today, men spend more money on computer games than they do on music. The huge growth in the sale of computer games has come about because of the boys who started playing games in the early 1980s and who never stopped. Boys are inducted into gaming culture at an early age and remain loyal members as they grow up. The industry recruits new game designers from their ranks. "A passion for games" is often explicit in job advertisements, and it goes without saying that the advertisers are seeking a passion for "real" games. And so it is that gaming culture reproduces itself.

It is this culture that sets games apart from other types of technology and other types of media. Gaming culture is unquestionably a male domain. It is "male," as in the opposite of "female." We mean this in the sense that the culture dichotomizes gender to the extreme. Conventional "real" games imagine gender as two fixed and stable categories that stand in stark contrast to one another. As a consequence, it is hard to conceive of the relation of games and gender without resorting to stereotypes. "Real" games value "victory over justice, competition over collaboration, speed over flexibility, transcendence over empathy, control over communication, and force over facilitation." And with gender so dichotomized, men become the norm, while women default to being the "other," the "ab-normal."

It is not easy to be the *other*. Still, women do choose to venture into the world of gaming. The women in our class, for example, do play "real" games. They play these games in spite of the fact that most of their girlfriends do not, in spite of the scarcity of female avatars, in spite of hackneyed portrayals of women as objects to be rescued, in spite of the fact that they do not normally fantasize about going to battle in a chain-mail bikini. Women venture into the world of gaming in spite of the constant reminders of their *otherness*. They do so because they *love* playing games and, especially, because they love to play "real" games. What is not clear is whether these women can be, or want to be, full citizens of the gaming culture—a culture in which they are configured as the *other* by definition, by exclusion, and by default.

Games for Girls and Women

In 1996, Mattel released *Barbie Fashion Designer*, which sold more than a million units. By gaming culture's standards *Barbie* was not really a game and, most certainly, it was not a "real" game. Nevertheless, it had a profound effect on the industry. It suggested that, contrary to conventional wisdom, girls would play on computers. The games industry responded with a "pink" games movement, scrambling to turn out games that would appeal to girls. None of these games were able to reproduce the success of *Barbie*. Within a year or two the in-

The Sims Is a Successful Girl Game

Girl gamers were largely hidden from view until *The Sims* brought them out in the 1990s. Created by legendary designer Will Wright for Electronic Arts, *The Sims* had a success with this hitherto untapped female market segment that came as a surprise to game-company executives. "We actually did not realize that women would gravitate to *Sims* as they did," says Virginia McArthur, a *Sims* producer. In focus groups, more than 50 percent of the *Sims* audience are teenage girls. The games have become a laboratory for studying gender roles in what might be called the relationship market.

The Sims games allow players to develop their own worlds from the ground up. "It's a gigantic sandbox," says McArthur. Instead of shooting enemies, you create characters and the environment in which they live from an array of options. The characters have needs—food, shelter, money, utilities—that must be met. "You order a pizza, you're going to have to go to the bathroom," McArthur says. Characters also want and need each other, especially in *The Sims 2* and its variants like *Nightlife*. "They have 'woohoo,'" she says. "That's our term for playing in bed."

Christopher Dickey and Nick Summers,
"A Female Sensibility," Newsweek International,
September 26, 2005.

dustry had backed off, deciding that "*Barbie* was a fluke," and that girls would not play computer games after all.

Barbie was indeed a fluke: the popularity of *Barbie Fashion Designer* reflects girls' interest in Barbie—not their interest in computer play. But to conclude that girls—and by extrapolation women—will not play computer games would be too hasty. Rather, we should ask why girls did not want to play these *particular* games. It might be that these were just not very good games. In trying to build games that would appeal to girls, "pink" game designers construed girls' games as the opposite of boys' games. Emphasizing justice over victory, collaboration over competition, flexibility over speed, empathy over transcendence, communication over control, and facilitation over force, these games may have lost some of their tension, their challenge, their edge.

Gender differences exist. As both the literature and incredulous parents report, there are—particularly at a young age—differences in play styles and game preferences between boys and girls. But differences do not necessarily translate into opposites. While most girls do not play American football, they do not necessarily want its reverse. They do play soccer—which is not opposite, but different. "Pink" game designers missed this point: they concocted a girly *antithesis* to boys' games, rather than coming up with an *alternative* that girls wanted to play.

What Games Do Women Want?

Who knows? There is no collective, shared aesthetic that captures "women's desires." But while there is no *everywoman*, research in the area of women and computer games all too often takes for granted that such a collective desire exists, again dichotomizing gender at the outset. Such research reinforces gender stereotypes rather than problematizing them.

Problematizing these stereotypes means to investigate whether the assumptions that we make about what women like and do not like are based on actual preferences, or whether these preferences are already informed and mediated by the stereotypes themselves. In other words, it means to understand gender dichotomization as an effect of—among other things—computer games, rather than taking them for granted as characterizations of women and men. It means to acknowledge that some women and not all men enjoy violent computer games or hyper-sexualized female characters. (As one of our students said in a class discussion: "I don't mind if they are hyper-sexualized, but please don't make them so stupid.") And it means to realize, as Graner Ray observes, that "girls and women are a market, not a genre."

Problematizing gender opens the way for new kinds of games: games that offer the possibility of acting against stereotype, games that play with conventional stereotypes to make them ironic and "strange," games that act as cultural critique.

Designing Alternative Games

To build these games, we need designers who can query gender stereotypes as they are building games. This is where a course such as our Gender and Computer Games comes in.

In their first game-building exercise in the course, teams of students experimented with gender connotations in games. They discovered that it is much easier to build in gender signifiers than to avoid them and that it requires thoughtful processing to eschew the suggestion of gender in characters and design. In another game-design exercise they were asked to take gender critique a step further and to design a game that plays with, and undermines, gender expectations.

This second exercise yielded interesting game variations. *Perfect Parent* is a first-person shooter in which the player, a James Bond-like character, is pulled out of retirement after twenty years to face an old arch-nemesis. The game is about balancing the battle against the arch-nemesis with cellphone calls from the protagonist's teenage children, who demand attention in increasingly intrusive ways.

Helpless Kittens is an online role-playing game in which players can choose their avatar from a list of stereotypes: for example, one can choose to be a feminist or a chauvinist. For each of these a series of roles signifies—and ironicizes—increasing power.

Galen is a retelling of the story of Perseus and Medusa from the perspective of Perseus's eleven-year-old sister, Galen. This tile-based adventure game, in the style of *King's Quest*, casts Perseus as a bumbling fool whose mistakes must be rectified by Galen. Onlookers credit Perseus with the solutions—and so the game explains how the character of the hero gets made.

While these games are just a start, they point to new directions. Each of them represents a thoughtful examination of gender-related issues in games, an examination that required the participation of *both* women and men.

We may not know what women want, but we do know that there are richer and more diverse games to come. We know that these games will appeal to both women and men. We know that they will disrupt rather than solidify gender stereotypes. We also know that they will be imagined by creative and insightful designers much like our students—maybe even our students—and that many of them will be women.

> "What is clear is that the game world is not, as so many assume, exclusively male; that female participation continues to increase; and that gender-role behavior is more nuanced than non-gamers tend to expect."

Video Games Transcend Gender Roles

John C. Beck and Mitchell Wade

The following viewpoint considers gaming from a business perspective. The authors describe a survey they conducted, the results of which indicated that video games can offer common ground for the sexes. They contend that men and women sometimes play games together and that in massive multiplayer online role-playing games, players often switch gender roles. John C. Beck is the president of the North Star Leadership Group and a senior research fellow at the Annenberg Center of the Digital Future at the University of Southern California. Mitchell Wade is the chief executive officer of CHOICE Humanitarian, a nonprofit organization.

As you read, consider the following questions:

1. According to the authors' survey, what percentage of gamers are women?

2. What types of games do the authors say men and women play later in life?

3. How do the authors say games introduce flexibility in gender roles?

It's hard to fault most professionals for missing the business potential of the game generation. As we've seen, the accident of video game history, just an issue of timing, has made overlooking games seem perfectly natural; one might almost say business as usual. When we [baby] boomers do pay attention to video games, it's usually with unaccustomed anxiety. The first things that pop to mind always seem to be negative: sexism, violence, stereotypes, and isolation.

As any labor economist will be quick to point out, changing gender roles can have huge economic impact. And most of us assume that the impact of video games on gender roles—so important in today's workforce—will be a disaster. It is easy to imagine some bleak scenarios. After all, games often present gender stereotypes so primitive that mainstream media at least claims to have forgotten them: men are hulking, muscle-bound members of elite tactical units (*Metal Gear Solid*), while women are chesty volleyball players (*Dead or Alive: Extreme Beach Volleyball*). In our survey, as well as in interviews with male and female college students and young professionals, we found significant differences in the way men and women play video games. In our interviews, men often reported that they thought women were much less interested in video games than they themselves were, and our survey data bore this out. Men, both older and younger, are much more likely than women to report that they played video games frequently as teenagers. But, interestingly enough, among our older respondents about the same percentage of women and men reported not playing games at all or that they were playing at a moderate level. The surprising difference really comes in respondents who are younger than thirty-four—the actual game generation. Here, even though more than 40 percent of all gamers are women, some 77 percent of women said they played few or no video games as teenagers.

Are video games another of those, gender-dividing activities, such as sports, that will keep the sexes from understanding each other once they come into close contact? What will gamers expect from each gender? Will all those grown-up adolescent boys want nothing more than a woman who looks like Lara Croft? Or someone as independent and competent as Lara Croft? Or will they only care about finding someone who knows all the secret codes to her game, *Tomb Raider?* Will they be able to handle the tension, failure, and messiness of a relationship? Or will they merely press reset every time the relationship hits a rocky point?

Males and Females Play Computer Games Together

Our interviews suggest that reality is more complex—and quite a bit more positive. To begin with, males and females play computer and video games together. More than thirty years after the inception of Title IX, the educational amendment that was supposed to bring gender equality to student athletics, real-life sports are still almost completely split by gender. Even now, a major ruckus can be raised by a woman playing in a PGA [Professional Golfers' Association] tournament, as Annika Sörenstam did in 2003. Beyond elementary school soccer, there are very few teams on which girls and boys actually play together.

Video games, on the other hand, are more and more a common ground for the sexes. Brothers and sisters will sit in the same room and play video games for hours on end. The

Gender Stereotyping

A study by [B.] Beasley and [T.] Collins-Standley (2002) looked at 341 Nintendo and PlayStation games to examine the presence and role of genders. Gender role stereotyping was based on the presence or absence of female characters and the types of clothing those characters were wearing in the games. They found that there were more characters of indeterminate gender than there were female characters and female characters were more likely to be seen in low-cut clothing and with bare arms than male characters, and approximately 40 percent of all female characters had disproportionately large chests.

Jami Barenthin and Marieke Van Puymbroeck,
"Research Update: The Joy Stick Generation,"
Parks & Recreation, *August 2006.*

girls may play less, but they are increasingly nearby. And as we saw earlier, female participation rates are going up. As kids move into the dating years, it is not at all uncommon for many teenagers on group dates to have a video game and pizza party where everyone (boys and girls alike) takes turns on the PlayStation. In college, students socialize around video game consoles—often playing video drinking games.

When we think about the way that games may change gender roles, the amount of game playing may be less important than the types of games played. The men in our survey reported that when they were teenagers, they tended to like the fast-twitch games that required speedy fingers and nerves of steel. Women were more likely to favor more cerebral arcade, quiz, and puzzle games. Later in life, both genders play a lot fewer arcade games (perhaps because that category of video game is increasingly less popular), replacing them with quiz and card games. But women are still much more likely to enjoy puzzles, whereas men still favor more strategy, sports, racing, and other fast-action games.

Games Go Beyond Sexual Stereotypes

There are also aspects of gaming that seem to go beyond sexual stereotypes—perhaps even bringing the genders together on some common ground. In a nonvirtual world, it would be rare to find teenage boys sitting around dressing and grooming a doll. Baby boomer boys could get away with such behaviors until they were about six years old. Then older male role models would intervene and tell them that it was "sissy" to be spending time dressing G.I. Joe. But in the video game world, almost every extreme sport, role-playing game, and, of course, simulation game (such as *The Sims*) includes long menus where players can choose the looks they want for the characters. Boy and girl players alike can try on thousands of different outfits, do their hair in different colors and styles, try on shoes, and experiment with facial hair. (Should it be any surprise, then, that a growing number of men in the United States can be categorized as "metrosexual"?) Then, after carefully adorning their virtual selves, teenage players (both male and female) venture out into the world of the video game and beat the pulp out of their opponents.

The interactivity of games introduces flexibility into gender roles as well. Boomer girls were socialized, in part, through hours of television. Our female colleagues often tell us that role models such as Samantha Stevens or June Cleaver often lurk somewhere in their subconscious. Boys, of course, have to deal with their inner Mannix, or maybe Captain Kirk. But the effect of games on these roles is potentially freeing in many ways. Players of either sex can experiment with gender roles in a way never before possible. Both boys and girls choose to play a vast array of female or male game characters. Even in our observation of young players—say, elementary school boys—we have heard surprisingly few negative comments about choosing to play a character of the opposite gender. It's tempting to imagine that this ability to choose a character of either gender who is just as strong, fast, smart, and likely to win as a character of the opposite gender instills in gamers the notion that anything is possible for either gender. A study at Nottingham Trent University found that 15 percent of the players in massively multiplayer online role-playing games, or MMPORPGs—a genre of games such as *EverQuest* in which the character you choose literally represents you to many other real humans—routinely switch genders.

When it comes to gender roles, games clearly haven't stopped evolving. MMPORPGs, for instance, have only been popular for a few years, compared to decades of conventional video game experience. What is clear is that the game world is not, as so many assume, exclusively male; that female participation continues to increase; and that gender-role behavior is more nuanced than nongamers tend to expect.

> *"It is wrong for anyone, child or adult, to spend long hours electronically rehearsing the prolonged agony and detailed humiliation of other human beings for their own amusement."*

Violent Video Games Are Bad for You

Jenny McCartney

In the following viewpoint, Jenny McCartney responds to a psychologist's report, Children in a Digital World, *which recommends stronger age ratings and more parental supervision. McCartney contends that even these recommendations are too mild. She claims that some video games, particularly those in which the player takes on the role of the wrongdoer, are wrong for anyone, child or adult, to play. McCartney is a columnist for London's* Telegraph.

As you read, consider the following questions:

1. What does McCartney say opinion-formers will use instead of morality as a basis for their considerations?

2. Does this author want to ban all video games?

Jenny McCartney, "There Is a Majority Against Vile Video Games, and It Is Moral," *Telegraph* (London), March 30, 2008. Copyright © Telegraph Media Group Limited 2008. Reproduced by permission.

3. Why does the author object to the "18 certificate"?

The report issued [in March of 2008] by [psychologist] Dr Tanya Byron on the effects of violent computer games upon young people was a typical well-meaning New Labour project: it made decent recommendations of dubious effectiveness. Dr Byron, a former television psychologist with experience of troubled children, said games should be rated by the user's age, and urged fines, even jail, for those selling them to underage children.

Dr Byron seems a sensible woman, and no doubt she has done her best to contain the spread of some of the more obnoxious material on offer without incurring the ire of the games lobby. But one of her remarks in an interview . . . struck me as particularly, and depressingly, modern. "My review is not about making any kind of moral pronouncements," she said, "although I do think that it is important to look at the desensitization to violence."

The f-word might be everywhere now, from playgrounds to the titles of BBC [British Broadcasting Corporation] documentaries, but it's the m-word that can render people really twitchy. Opinion-formers will squirm to avoid an argument that is seen to be based on moral considerations: they will grope instead for the comfort-blanket of scientific data, and "pragmatic approaches", and "natural concerns".

The word "moral" still has deeply unfashionable associations with Mary Whitehouse [a British woman who campaigned for morality in broadcast media], and the "moral majority" protesting against the "tide of filth" in books and television in the United States. How tame and inoffensive that tide looks now.

Yet the truth, surely, is that the majority of us would indeed recoil from the idea that our teenage son or daughter was upstairs playing *Manhunt 2*, a recently licensed game in which the protagonist, an escaper from an experimental asylum, tortures and murders other players in the most graphic ways.

It might well be true, as we are so often told, that most children who immerse themselves daily in violent video games will not go on to commit real murder. For that, I suppose, we must all be grateful.

Violent Video Games Are Morally Wrong

But the instinctive objection remains, and it is indeed rooted in morality: the sense that it is wrong for anyone, child or adult, to spend long hours electronically rehearsing the prolonged agony and detailed humiliation of other human beings for their own amusement. It is insidiously corrupting to their view of themselves and other people.

No one is saying that all video games are damaging, even if they depict fighting. I am not under the illusion that we can, or should, attempt to confine older children to a play world made up entirely of group hugs and communal co-operation. A significant vogue in video-games, however, is to put the player not in the role of a character who combats wrongdoing, but of the wrongdoers themselves: the mass murderer, the torturer, the street thug, drug dealer or pimp.

The selection of protagonist is no doubt ironic, with these strutting miscreants representing the fantasies of nerdy little middle-class boys, but when one considers the prevalence of gangs, drug dealers and teenage violence on the streets the irony doesn't seem quite so amusing.

The authorities have found themselves powerless to oppose the nastiest examples of such "entertainment". Consider *Manhunt 2*, a game so repellent that the British Board of Film Classifications [BBFC] sought to ban it. The BBFC is certainly no bastion of old-fashioned censorship—the *Guardian* recently said it was more like a "progressive young uncle" than a "strict matron".

But even the progressive young uncle was shocked by *Manhunt 2*. David Cooke, the BBFC's director, banned the game for its "unrelenting focus on stalking and brutal slaying", adding that it was distinguished by its encouragement of "sustained and cumulative casual sadism". The fact that, in America, the makers cut a castration-with-pliers scene for its Wii version gives you some idea of its content.

The BBFC's ruling was repeatedly overturned by the Video Appeals Committee, and the game was licensed for sale in Britain. . . . It has an "18" certificate [which can be purchased only by someone 18 or older], but it would only require an 18-year-old player with younger siblings to leave it lying around at home, for it to be freely available to underage players.

This is a curious country, in which it is socially acceptable to be outraged by bottled water and plastic bags, but embarrassingly *de trop* to get worked up about sickening depictions of violence as entertainment.

Perhaps if more people, including teenagers, were prepared to voice moral objections to this toxic stuff, it would no longer be possible to lampoon them for caring.

> *"If people are to nurture their souls, they need to feel a sense of control, meaningfulness, even expertise in the face of risk and complexity. . . . Good video games are, in this sense, food for the soul."*

Video Games Are Good for Your Soul

James Paul Gee

In the following viewpoint, author James Paul Gee argues that video games are good for the soul. He describes a "good" video game, defines one's "soul," and then explains how he sees gaming to be good for the soul. He also refutes the common accusations that video games promote violence. Gee is the Tashia Morgridge Professor of Reading at the University of Wisconsin-Madison. He has written extensively on the subject of video games and learning.

As you read, consider the following questions:

1. How does Gee describe "good" video games?

James Paul Gee, *Good Video Games + Good Learning.* New York: Peter Lang, 2007. Copyright © 2007 Peter Lang Publishing, Inc., New York. All rights reserved. Reproduced by permission.

2. According to the author, what kinds of pleasure come from good video games?

3. Why is Gee not concerned about video games as a cause of violence?

Good video games are good for your soul. Now there's a statement that begs for some qualifications!

First, what's a video game? What I mean are the sorts of commercial games people play on computers and game platforms like the PlayStation 2, the GameCube, the Xbox, and the handheld Game Boy. I mean action, adventure, shooter, strategy, sports, and role-playing games. I mean games like *Castlevania, Half-Life, Deus Ex, Metal Gear Solid, Max Payne, Return to Castle Wolfenstein, Tony Hawk's Underground, Rise Rise of Nations, Civilization, Age of Mythology, The Elder Scrolls III: Morrowind, Allied Assault, Call of Duty, Tales of Symphonia, ICO, Pikmin, Zelda: The Wind Waker,* and *Ninja Gaiden* to name some random good games off the top of my head. There are many others.

Second, what does "good for you" mean? Next to nothing is good or bad for you in and of itself and all by itself. It all depends on how it is used and the context in which it is used. Is television good or bad for children? Neither and both. It's good if people around them are getting them to think and talk about what they are watching, bad when they sit there alone, watching passively, being baby-sat by the tube. The same is true of books. Reading reflectively, asking yourself questions, and engaging in a dialogue with others, is good for your head. Believing everything you read uncritically is bad for you and for the rest of us, as well, since you may well become a danger to the world.

Good and Bad Video Games

So good video games are good for your soul when you play them with thought, reflection, and engagement with the world around you. They are good if, as a player, you begin to think and act like a game designer while you play the game, something good games encourage. After all, players co-author games by playing them, since if the player doesn't interact with the game and make choices about what will happen, nothing will happen. Each page of a book and each scene in a movie is predetermined before you see it and is the same for every reader. Many acts and their order in a video game, however, are open to player choice and are different for different players.

So, then, what's a good, as opposed to a bad, video game? You have to play the games. Good games are the ones gamers come to see as "gaming goodness," "fair," and sometimes even "deep"—all terms of gaming art. Good games are the games that lots of gamers come to agree are good, though they rarely think any one game is perfect.

Some games, like *ICO* or *American McGee's Alice*, get discovered late and become underground classics, while others, like *Half-Life* or *Zelda: The Wind Waker*, nearly everyone agrees from the outset are good. Then there are games like *Anachronox*, which didn't sell well and received some rather tepid reviews, but is, I'm telling you, a darn good game—you see I have my own opinions about these matters. In fact, different gamers like and dislike different games and different types of games.

Defining the Soul

OK, then, what for heaven's sake is your soul? And what could playing video games have to do with it? Once, years ago, I had the special experience of going back into time and living for several years in the Middle Ages. The details need not detain us—you'll just have to trust me on this—but, believe me, that experience taught me what souls meant in one context. That is not what I mean here.

Too often in the world today people from all sorts of religions believe that those who don't share their beliefs will go to some sort of hell and, worse, they are sometimes willing to make life hell for others here and now to help them, whether they like it or not, avoid going to hell. Or, perhaps, they just make life hell for others to ensure that they themselves will go to heaven, having displayed their merit by removing a suitable number of infidels. While I do retain a certain nostalgia for the Middle Ages, that nostalgia plays no role in this book.

So what could I mean by "soul?" I mean what the poet Emily Dickinson meant:

My life closed twice before its
close—
It yet remains to see
If Immortality unveil
A third event to me
So huge, so hopeless to conceive
As these that twice befell.
Parting is all we know of heaven,
And all we need of hell.

What Emily Dickinson is talking about here is not the immortality, heaven, and hell of traditional religion (Dickinson was skeptical of traditional religion at a time and place where that was socially dangerous, especially for women). She is talking about a fact that every human being knows and feels, a fact that defines what it means to be human. This fact is that we each have two parts. One of these parts is our body. If you truly traumatize the body, it will die and it can die but once, which is, indeed, a mercy.

But there is another part of us, a part to which different religions and cultures through the ages have given different names. This part—let's just say it is our "soul"—can be traumatized over and over again and not die, just as in the case of the two emotionally damaging events to which Emily Dickin-

Puzzle and Word Games Increase Mental Ability and Relieve Stress

[In the words of psychologist Carl G. Arinoldo:] The casual word/puzzle games tend to provide a wonderful avenue for the players to exercise and enhance their concentration and focusing abilities. Problem-solving and decision-making skills also appear to be enhanced. . . . In addition, studies seem to be showing that playing these types of games can help to keep the healthy brain active and vital. In fact, people have reported that they feel more "mentally alert" after a session with one of these games.

Aside from the cognitive benefits, playing the casual puzzle/word games help people in reducing their stress. By concentrating and focusing on the game, a person can take a "mental vacation" from whatever it is at the moment that is causing stress in his or her life.

Janene Mascarella, "Get Your Game On!"
Long Island Exchange, *September 21, 2007.*

son alludes. No mercy here, as we all very well know, unless you have been very fortunate, indeed, in your life. The rest of us have, if old enough, already died more than once. This part—this soul—is immortal in the sense that, until the body goes, it can go on suffering grievously over and over again, suffering many deaths, unlike the body which can die but once.

Heaven and Hell on Earth

But it is because we have this soul part that events and other people can take on such a charge for human beings. It is because we have this soul part that events and other people can

give us what we know of heaven here on earth. It is only because losing a loved one, either by death or parting, as Dickinson is alluding to, can give rise to such pain that loving others can rise to such joy. You can't really have the one without
the other. Having the charge, the spark, is heaven and losing it
is hell. But you can't have it if there is no chance of losing it,
that's the way of life for us humans. That's why we "need"
hell. There is no heaven without hell, no positive charges
without risk of negative ones.

Emily Dickinson very well knew, then, that it matters
hugely whether life here and now for people is heaven or hell.
It matters hugely whether we help make life heaven or hell for
others, whether we murder or rejoice their other parts, their
souls, that part of them that cannot die as long as they have
their bodies. It matters. We can be complicit with murder
without having killed anyone. The world can murder us several times over long before it takes our bodies.

The Middle Ages saw to it that peasants and the poor died
many times before they died. The rich got off more easily;
though, by the nature of life itself, they, too, paid their soul
dues. Modern life offers more opportunities, but more complexity, as well. For many people—perhaps, all of us at times—
modern life offers too much risk and too much complexity.
We don't really understand what's going on around us, lots of
it just doesn't make any good sense, at least as far as we can
tell. We can understand why some people turn to fundamen-
talism to garner secure "truths" without thought and reflection. It is, indeed, an attempt to save their souls, to protect
themselves from the traumas of modern life, a life where often
the rich get richer, the poor get poorer, and everyone suffers
risks created by other people, even people clear across the
globe.

If people are to nurture their souls, they need to feel a
sense of control, meaningfulness, even expertise in the face of
risk and complexity. They want and need to feel like heroes in

their own life stories and to feel that their stories make sense. They need to feel that they matter and that they have mattered in other people's stories. If the body feeds on food, the soul feeds on agency and meaningfulness. I argue that good video games are, in this sense, food for the soul, particularly appropriate food in modern times. Of course, the hope is that this food will empower the soul to find agency and meaning in other aspects of life.

Good Video Games Create Learning and Pleasure

Good video games give people pleasures. These pleasures are connected to control, agency, and meaningfulness. But good games are problem-solving spaces that create deep learning, learning that is better than what we often see today in our schools. Pleasure and learning: For most people these two don't seem to go together. But that is a mistruth we have picked up at school, where we have been taught that pleasure is fun and learning is work, and, thus, that work is not fun. But, in fact, good videos games are hard work and deep fun. So is good learning in other contexts.

Pleasure is the basis of learning for humans and learning is, like sex and eating, deeply pleasurable for human beings. Learning is a basic drive for humans. School has taught people to fear and avoid learning as anorexics fear and avoid food; it has turned some people into mental anorexics. Some of these same people learn deeply in and through games, though they say they are playing, not learning. The other people who often say they are playing when they're working hard at learning are those professionals—scientists, scholars, and craftsmen—who love their work. . . .

Well, we have to deal with it. We all know the topic is looming over us. What about violence and video games? Does playing video games lead people to be more violent? More ink has been devoted to this topic than any other concerned with video games. But most of that ink has been wasted.

The 19th century was infinitely more violent than the 20th in terms of crime (though not actual warfare) and no one played video games. The politicians who have heretofore sent people to war have not played video games—they're too old. The Japanese play video games more than Americans do, as, indeed, they watch more television, but their society is much less violent than America's. No, as we said above, video games are neither good nor bad all by themselves, they lead neither to violence nor to peace. They can be and do one thing in one family, social, or cultural context, quite another in other such contexts.

Real Violence Is More Complex than Influential Media

If you want to lower violence, then worry about those contexts, which all extend well beyond just playing video games. Politicians who get hot and heavy about violence in video games usually don't want to worry about such contexts—contexts like poverty, bad parenting, and a culture that celebrates greed, war, and winning. Too expensive, perhaps. In my view, the violence and video games question is a silly one and you won't hear much more about it here. I do live in fear of people who would kill someone because they have played a video game, but I know that they would equally kill someone if they had read a book or seen a movie or even overheard another nut, and I would like you first to take their weapons away. Then, too, someone should have taught these people how to play video games, read books, and watch movies critically and reflectively.

In a world in which millions of people across the globe are dying in real wars, many of them civil wars, it is surely a luxury that we can worry about little boys getting excited for ten minutes after playing a shooter. There are much better things to worry about and I just pray that a time comes in the world where such a problem really merits serious attention. Let's stop the killing, for example in Africa, on the part of people who have never played a video game before we ban games, books, and movies to save ourselves from a handful of disturbed teenagers who would have been better served by better families and schools.

On a more positive note, we should realize that the possibilities of video games and the technologies by which they are made are immense. Video games hold out immense economic opportunities for business and for careers. They hold out equally immense possibilities for the transformation of learning inside and outside schools. They hold out immense promise for changing how people think, value, and live. We haven't seen the beginning yet. As I write, all the game platforms are on their last legs, soon to be replaced by more powerful devices. What wonderful worlds will we eventually see? What charged virtual lives will we be able to live?

The Wild West and space were seen as new frontiers. Video games and the virtual worlds to which they give birth are, too, a new frontier and we don't know where they will lead. It would be a shame, indeed, not to find out because, like any frontier, they were fraught with risk and the unknown. But, then, I have already admitted that all of us in the complex modern world are frightened of risk and the unknown. But that, I will argue, is a disease of the soul that good games can help alleviate, though, of course, not cure.

Some people may say, well, he's really arguing it's all about escape from the perils and pitfalls of real life. But, then, I will say there are escapes that lead nowhere, like hard drugs, and escapes like scholarly reflection and gaming that can lead to the imagination of new worlds, new possibilities to deal with those perils and pitfalls, new possibilities for better lives for everyone. Our emotions and imagination—our souls—need food for the journeys ahead.

Periodical Bibliography

The following articles have been selected to supplement the diverse views presented in this chapter.

Verena Dobnik	"Surgeons May Err Less by Playing Video Games," *Associated Press*, April 7, 2004.
Mike Drummond	"Do Video Games Make You Smarter, Stronger, Faster? Hell Yeah!" *Inventors Digest*, August 2008.
Jill Duffy	"Casual Play May Be Good for What Ails You," *Game Developer*, May 2006.
Jeff Green	"Gray Power," *Games for Windows*, April 1, 2007.
Jeff Green	"The Peggle Disease: When Casual Gaming Stops Being Casual," *Games for Windows*, March 2008.
Jane McGonigal	"Gaming Science," *Seed*, January/February 2008.
Jane McGonigal	"Video Games Are Training People to Solve Tough, Real-World Problems," *Christian Science Monitor*, November 5, 2007.
Jennifer Ordoñez	"A Most Casual Addiction," *Newsweek*, May 5, 2008.
Lisa Pickoff-White	"Video Games: Sexist Tendencies," *UPI Perspectives*, February 14, 2005.
The Science Teacher	"Video Games and the Brain," April–May 2008.

OPPOSING
VIEWPOINTS®
SERIES

CHAPTER 3

What Is the Impact of Violence in Video Games?

Chapter Preface

In April 1999, two high school students in Columbine, Colorado, Eric Harris and Dylan Klebold, opened fire on Columbine High School, killing twelve students and one teacher and injuring twenty-three others before killing themselves. Both boys were avid players of video games such as *Doom* and *Wolfenstein 3D*. Some people blamed the incident on the games, claiming that the whole massacre was rehearsed while playing *Doom*. In April 2007, Seung-Hui Cho, a student at Virginia Polytechnic Institute and State University, killed thirty-two people and injured many others before committing suicide in a shooting spree at the university. Some said video games were responsible for this massacre, also, although no evidence was found to support the theory that Cho was a gamer.

Video games have been accused of causing these and other incidents of real-world violence. Supporters of this theory say that violence in video games is worse than in television or movies because the game player actively participates in violent acts during the game. Even the name of one popular genre of games, "first-person shooter," points to the personal involvement of the player in the violent acts that take place. Some studies indicate that young people show increased aggression after playing this type of game.

Others disagree with this point of view, some going as far as claiming that participating in violent games is a release for aggressive feelings that might otherwise be acted out in the real world. They cite statistics that point to lower incidences of violent crime since video games began. They contend that the increased levels of aggression that are indicated by some studies do not prove a causal relationship between playing games and violent acts; they theorize that people with aggressive tendencies may be drawn to such games, but that the games did not provoke such tendencies.

The viewpoints in the following chapter examine both sides of this argument and consider the pros and cons of using video games to train the military and depicting recent real-world battles in video games.

| "High levels of exposure to violent video games have been linked to forms of physically violent behavior, as well as other less extreme types of aggression."

Violent Video Games Cause Aggression

Craig A. Anderson

The following viewpoint is from an expert opinion on media and video game violence presented in a court case in a United States District Court of Illinois. The author, Craig A. Anderson, has extensive experience in the field of psychology, particularly in the areas of aggression and media violence. Anderson summarizes research findings about media violence in general and video game violence in particular. He states that exposure to violence in video games is more detrimental than exposure to violence in television or movies, and he highlights some of the ways in which video games cause aggression.

As you read, consider the following questions:

1. According to Anderson, what are the long-term effects of exposure to media violence?

Craig A. Anderson, *Declaration of Craig A. Anderson, Ph.D., in United States District Court, Northern District of Illinois, Eastern Division*, October 5, 2005.

2. What does the author say are the effects of exposure to violent video games?

3. How does the author believe the long-term effects of repeated exposure to media violence are caused?

The research literature on the effects of exposure to media violence is one of the largest, most diverse in methods, and most well understood (by true experts) in all of social and behavioral science. There have been numerous reviews by a variety of expert panels and commissions, all coming to the same conclusion that exposure to media violence is a risk factor for aggression and violence. Researchers using modern meta-analytic techniques to statistically combine the results of all relevant empirical studies also generally come to the same conclusion. The next sections summarize these effects.

In July of 2000, representatives of six major professional health societies issued a "Joint Statement on the Impact of Entertainment Violence on Children" at a Congressional Public Health Summit. The groups included: American Academy of Pediatrics, American Academy of Child & Adolescent Psychiatry, American Psychological Association, American Medical Association, American Academy of Family Physicians, and the American Psychiatric Association.

The Statement notes (among other things) that, "Television, movies, music, and interactive games are powerful learning tools, and highly influential media." It lists four main types of effects of exposure to violent entertainment media:

- Children who see a lot of violence are more likely to view violence as an effective way of settling conflicts. Children exposed to violence are more likely to assume that acts of violence are acceptable behavior.

- Viewing violence can lead to emotional desensitization towards violence in real life. It can decrease the likelihood that one will take action on behalf of a victim when violence occurs.

- Entertainment violence feeds a perception that the world is a violent and mean place. Viewing violence increases fear of becoming a victim of violence, with a resultant increase in self-protective behaviors and a mistrust of others.

- Viewing violence may lead to real-life violence. Children exposed to violent programming at a young age have a higher tendency for violent and aggressive behavior later in life than children who are not so exposed.

In August of 2005, the American Psychological Association (APA) passed a "Resolution on Violence in Video Games and Interactive Media." Among other things, the resolution notes that there is considerable evidence of harmful effects of exposure to violent video games, similar to harmful effects found previously in studies of television and film violence. The resolution also suggests that violent video games may be more conducive to learning harmful lessons than violent television, and calls for a reduction of all violence in video games and interactive media marketed to children and youth. . . .

The Effects of Media Violence

It is important to note the differences between short-term versus long-term effects. Short-term effects are those that occur almost immediately upon exposure. Some of them may last only a short time (minutes or hours), whereas others may persist for a considerably longer time. The short-term effects of most relevance to this case are:

- Observational learning of how to aggress.

- Increase in aggressive behavior.

- Increase in aggressive thinking.

- Increase in aggressive emotions.

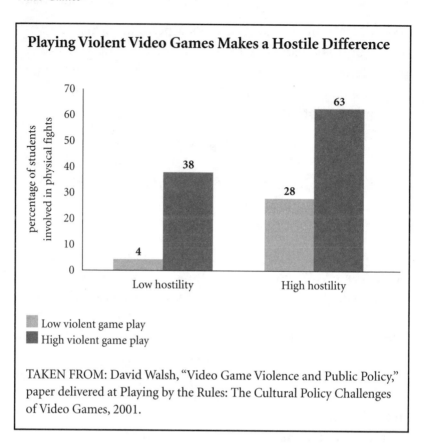

Playing Violent Video Games Makes a Hostile Difference

TAKEN FROM: David Walsh, "Video Game Violence and Public Policy,"
paper delivered at Playing by the Rules: The Cultural Policy Challenges
of Video Games, 2001.

It is generally believed by media violence researchers that
the last three of these four short-term effects of exposure usually dissipate fairly quickly. However, once one learns how to
commit a specific behavior by observing someone else doing
it, that knowledge is unlikely to disappear. Whether it becomes a frequently used part of the observer's behavioral repertoire depends on several factors, including whether the observed behavior itself was rewarded in some way (for example,
did the screen character get what he/she wanted by his violent
action), and, whether the observer is rewarded or punished
when he/she uses a similar type of aggressive action.

Even those short-term effects that dissipate fairly quickly
are important because they provide an additional basis for

long-term effects. For example, highly stable attitudes towards violence, beliefs about the effectiveness of violent behavior and its appropriateness, attitudes towards particular groups of people (e.g., women, police, prostitutes, criminals, Muslims) are unlikely to emerge from one brief exposure to media violence that illustrates or supports those attitudes and beliefs, even though short-term changes in such thinking does occur. But any factor that repeatedly induces a particular set of attitudes, beliefs, and other thought processes increases the likelihood that they will become internalized, or more permanent ways of viewing the world. In other words, it is useful to view each media violence exposure as a type of practice or learning opportunity.

Long-term effects are those that result from repeated exposure to media violence. The most relevant long-term effects of repeated exposure to violent media are:

- Increase in the likelihood of aggressive behavior, including violent behavior (various types of physical assault).

- Increase in positive attitudes, beliefs, and thought processes concerning aggression.

- Reduction of normal inhibitions against aggression.

The evidence concerning who is most vulnerable to media violence exposure is somewhat mixed. There is some evidence that initially aggressive individuals, younger children, or males might be more affected than relatively non-aggressive individuals, older children, or females. But these moderating effects are not consistent, and many studies find significant effects of media violence on non-aggressive individuals, older youths (including young adults), and females. In other words, no specific group has repeatedly demonstrated total immunity to aggression-related effects of exposure to media violence.

Media Violence Is Not Alone in Its Influence

The research evidence on the overall effects of media violence is consistent across all three of the major types of research designs: randomized experiments, cross-sectional correlational studies, and longitudinal studies.

Three additional points of relevance warrant consideration. First, human aggression, especially the most extremely violent forms of it, is influenced by many risk and resilience factors. A partial listing includes a history of antisocial or aggressive behavior, positive attitudes and beliefs about aggression, maladaptive parenting styles, weapon availability, low IQ, neighborhood crime, and antisocial peers. Second, extremely violent behaviors usually emerge only when several risk factors are in place. Media violence exposure is one such risk factor, perhaps the one that is easiest to modify. Third, the best understanding of violent video game effects arises from consideration of research and research-based theoretical models on all types of media violence (television, film, video games, etc.), as well as basic research and theory on human learning and developmental processes.

The research literature on violent video games is necessarily smaller and more recent than the research on violent television and film. Nonetheless, recent meta-analytic reviews of the research give rise to the following conclusions. Exposure to violent video games:

- Increases aggressive behavior.

- Increases aggressive thinking.

- Increases aggressive emotions.

- Increases physiological arousal.

- Decreases prosocial (or helping) behavior.

Furthermore, high levels of exposure to violent video games have been linked to forms of physically violent behavior, as well as other less extreme types of aggression. These effects appear to be about the same size for males and females, younger versus older youths, and more versus less generally aggressive individuals. However, more research is needed before strong conclusions can be drawn about whether some groups might be more vulnerable than others. . . .

Video Gaming Involves Violent Activity

It is interesting to note that whereas television viewing time by children and adolescents appears to not be changing much, time spent on video games has been increasing. Currently there is only one published study that directly tests whether violent video game exposure is more detrimental than violent movie or television exposure. In a correlational study [Jeanne B.] Funk found that high exposure to violent video games was associated with lower levels of empathy and more positive attitudes towards violence. Television violence did not independently contribute to either empathy or attitudes towards violence. Movie violence was significantly associated only with attitudes towards violence. In addition to this one study, there is at least one unpublished study in progress showing similar results. Furthermore, there are strong theoretical reasons to believe that violent video game exposure could have a stronger impact on the player than violent television or movie exposure.

Previous research has demonstrated that learning increases when people are more actively involved in the task. Playing a video game is a highly active activity that requires constant attention from the player, while watching television is a fairly passive activity. The continuation of the game depends on the player's alertness and responses, while a television show continues to be broadcast regardless of what the viewer is doing in the room. This difference between video games and television would suggest that violent video game exposure may enhance learning aggressive behaviors, attitudes, and beliefs compared to an equivalent amount of exposure to violent television.

Past research has shown that identifying oneself with a violent character can increase the effect of the media violence exposure. Television viewers might or might not identify with the violent characters in the program; however, this is not the case for violent video game players. Violent video game players are required to assume the identity of a violent character. In some games, commonly referred to as first person shooters, the players see the world from the violent character's visual perspective. In "third person" games, players can often select the gender, appearance, and abilities of the character who they control. Often, characters can be adjusted to create an electronic likeness of the player. In other games, players can download images (called "skins") into the game and overlay these images onto the character model in the game. These skins can be pictures of players themselves, thereby electronically embedding their visual likeness into the game. Once again, these differences between violent video games and violent television would suggest that violent video game exposure could have a larger impact on players compared to violent television exposure.

Some of the most cited research in psychology shows that behavior (including aggressive behavior) is increased when the behaviors are rewarded. In violent television programs and films, reward for violent actions is indirect. Viewers' "reward" for a violent character's action is seeing the result of that action (e.g., witnessing the character receive something he or she wants, the death of his or her enemy . . .). However, in violent video games, rewards are much more direct. Players instantaneously receive numerous types of reward for their own actions in the game (e.g., points, access to new levels of the game, abilities to use new weapons, intriguing video and audio effects, verbal praise such as a voice saying "nice shot" or "you're unstoppable"). Because rewards in violent video games are more numerous and more direct than in violent television or films, this suggests violent video game exposure may be more detrimental.

Research has demonstrated that the media violence effect is cumulative. That is, exposure to more media violence increases the effect. Violent television programs and movies do not display violent actions constantly. A large portion of time in movies and television programs are allotted to plot development, romantic storylines, and comedic relief. Many violent video games, however, almost continuously display violence. Often, the player is constantly searching for new enemies, engaging them in combat, and being rewarded for violent actions. Because of this difference, violent video game players are exposed to more scenes of violence compared to an equivalent amount of time with violent television or films.

Violent Video Games Increase Aggression

Short-term effects, those that occur during and for at least a short time after playing a violent video game, are believed to be the result of increases in the accessibility of aggressive thought, aggressive affect, and/or physiological arousal. Playing a violent video game can increase any of these three types of variables, each of which has a long history in theoretical models of human aggression.

Long-term effects of repeated exposure to media violence are believed to be the result of changes (learning) in a wide array of aggression-related variables, ranging from such obvious variables as simple knowledge about how to harm others to less obvious variables such as the chronic accessibility of aggressive thoughts and scripts. When a person plays a violent video game, several things are occurring. First, players are witnessing scenes of violence, which make aggressive thoughts more readily accessible in the player. Also, aggressive scripts for situations involving confrontation are being introduced and reinforced. Aggressive scripts are essentially abstract guidelines for how to behave in certain situations. When aggressive thoughts and scripts are more accessible in memory, they tend to lead people to interpret events that occur to them in a more hostile way, which in turn tends to increase the likelihood of an aggressive behavior. The chronic accessibility of any type of thoughts and scripts is affected by how often those thoughts and scripts have been used in the past, by repetition. Other types of aggression-related variables believed to be involved in long term media violence effects include: aggressive beliefs and attitudes; aggression-biased perceptual schemas; and aggressive expectation schemas. Finally, it is believed that repeated media violence exposure can lead to decreases in normal aggression-inhibitions, such as desensitization of normal negative emotional reactions to violence.

| *"In 2005 . . . just 12 percent of the videogames sold were violent enough to bear an M-rating [mature] by the Entertainment Software Ratings Board, the industry's voluntary ratings group."*

Violent Video Games Do Not Cause Aggression

David Kushner

The following viewpoint is a response to reports of studies linking violent video games to aggression. The author, David Kushner, claims that the behavior called "aggression" in these studies is not related to criminal violent activity. He also criticizes studies for using old games rather than recent ones and for studying play for only a short period of time. He concludes that, although a link between video games and what the researchers define as "aggression" may exist, there is no causal link between violent games and violent criminal activity. Kushner is an author and editor and serves as an adjunct professor of journalism at New York University.

David Kushner, "Off Target," *Electronic Gaming Monthly*, August 2007, pp. 12–16. Copyright © 2007 Ziff Davis Publishing Holdings Inc. All rights reserved. Reproduced by permission.

As you read, consider the following questions:

1. According to the author, how do researchers measure aggression?

2. What other pastimes does Kushner think could be linked to aggression if they were studied?

3. What does the British Board of Film Classification survey, as quoted by Kushner, reveal about game violence?

We can assume two things about you if you're reading this magazine [*Electronic Gaming Monthly*]: You don't think playing violent videogames can make someone go aggro [aggressive behavior] in real life, and you haven't authored any studies linking violent games to violent behavior. But the people who *do believe* and *have authored* such studies have gotten a lot of play lately in the mainstream media—and they're putting the future of your favorite pastime at risk.

Following the April 16 [2007] Virginia Tech shootings, the *Washington Post* reported online that the killer had a history of playing the PC squad-based multiplayer shooter *Counter-Strike*. By the time the paper took down the reference from its website the next day (due, the writer later said, to a necessary update), it was too late. Ubiquitous antigame crusader Jack Thompson raised the specter on CNN. Dr. Phil played the blame game on *Larry King Live*. "The mass murderers of tomorrow are the children of today that are being programmed with this massive violence overdose," he said.

Then on April 26, the Federal Communications Commission [FCC] weighed in with its report, three years in the making, on the impact of media violence (particularly television violence) on kids. It suggests that Congress can step in to protect kids from harm by regulating violence on TV without violating the First Amendment. The thought of the Feds legislating videogames strikes many as dangerous. The American Civil Liberties Union [ACLU] calls it "political pandering."

Howard Stern calls Dr. Phil an a-hole. Once again, the debate that has run from Columbine to Blacksburg continues to rage. And when it does, each side looks to the same place to buttress their arguments: scientific research on the effects of violent videogames. But with sensational media and political distortion in the way, getting to the truth of the research is the trickiest game of all.

Defining Aggression

At the end of the day, scientists—including those behind the studies cited in the FCC report—still aren't sure if playing violent games leads to real-life violence at all. "The research doesn't support the notion that [playing violent games] leads to aggression," says Dr. Jonathan Freedman, a psychologist from the University of Toronto. "It doesn't even deal with the question of whether it leads to criminal violent behavior or real violence. At most, it addresses the question of whether it leads to aggression, which I don't think it does."

One of the problems with the studies is how the term "aggression" is defined. "The missing element is that most of these studies, if you look at them just a little bit critically, don't really measure what a lot of people purport they're measuring, and people don't understand how they fall short," says sociologist Dr. Karen Sternheimer of the University of Southern California and author of *Kids These Days: Facts and Fictions About Today's Youth*. While the general public equates aggression with violent behavior, actual violent behavior has never been measured—for obvious reasons. "We can't have people assault, rape, or murder someone" in the lab, says Dr. Brad Bushman, a University of Michigan psychologist who studies the effects of media violence. Instead, researchers are left to measure innocuous examples of so-called aggressive behavior—behavior that doesn't remotely resemble criminally violent activity. This has ranged from having subjects punch an inflatable Bozo doll to, more commonly, blast opponents with a loud noise.

Even Dr. Karen Dill, who with Dr. Craig Anderson coauthored one of the most-cited studies—2000's "Video Games and Aggressive Thoughts, Feelings, and Behavior in the Laboratory and in Life"—admits "hearing the noise is not harmful." Nevertheless, the report opens with an allusion to Columbine and purports that "one possible contributing factor is violent games." To many, that's an egregious leap. "Pressing a button that delivers a short burst of loud noise is pretty remote from real aggression," Freedman notes.

Studies Use Old Games

But it's not just the measures of aggression that are questionable—it's the means through which participant reactions are elicited in the first place. Reading the fine print in the Dill and Anderson study, for example, reveals that the researchers used outdated, mismatched games and required an absurdly brief amount of actual playtime from the subjects. The researchers compared the response to people playing two games released in the early 1990s: *Wolfenstein 3D*, the first first-person shooter, and the puzzle adventure *Myst*. The disparity between the game styles raises questions about the results. Though the goal of the study is to explore the effect of violent games on aggression, a shooter is sure to elicit more aggressive behavior than a puzzle game. It's like comparing apples to hand grenades. Wouldn't it have been better to compare two action games—one with violence and one without?

The study required 32 undergrads to play the games for 15 minutes each. They were then given the opportunity to send a noise blast to an opponent—often just a computer proxy—after they finished the game. "You can't study people for 20 minutes and know what's going to happen to people in society 10 years later," says Dr. Dmitri Williams of the University of Illinois at Urbana-Champaign. Williams recently authored one of the first long-term studies, in which he observed players of the online PC role-playing-game *Asheron's Call* for more than 56 hours in a period of a month. His results? "I found no evidence of increased aggression or aggressive attitudes," he says.

Dr. Patrick Markey, a psychology professor at Villanova University, decided to take another perspective: studying what role a person's anger level *before* playing a game has on the aggressive behavior coming out. And Markey, unlike some of his colleagues, actually uses games played in the last decade. The 167 students who participated played games such as *Doom 3* and *Project Gotham Racing*. His conclusion: The people who had previously filled out questionnaires reflecting an even-keel personality were less aggro after playing a violent game. Those who had a more aggressive disposition were more susceptible to these heightened emotions.

While some could conclude in broad strokes that games cause aggression, the nuances tell another story, Markey notes. "The general research shows there is an effect of violent games on aggression, but what gets lost is [that] this effect isn't that big," he says. And, of course, videogames aren't the only pastimes that could lead to aggression: dodgeball, paintball, and a bad beat in *Texas Hold 'Em* can heighten arousal, too. Dr. Vincent Mathews, a radiologist at Indiana University who has studied the brain's response to violent videogames, suggests that the effects of these other activities would be comparable. "I would think that paintball or dodgeball would show similar results," he says. But no one is calling for these games to be banned.

No Causal Link Between Games and Violence

Critics of violent games cite the studies as further proof that media violence leads to murder. As Thompson wrote in March 2007, "The American Psychological Association [APA] in Au-

Evidence Does Not Support Video Games' Violent Influence

Statistical data illustrate that violence in children has, in fact, decreased during the time video games have been played. The DOJ [Department of Justice] states: "Offending rates for [homicide by] children under age 14 increased in the late 1980s and early 1990s, but have recently fallen to the lowest levels recorded." Thus, since the release of *Mortal Kombat* and *Doom* in 1992 and 1994, respectively, the rates of both violent crimes and homicides committed by children have decreased sharply. If games like *Mortal Kombat* and *Doom* cause violence in children, then why is the rate of violent crimes committed by children at an all-time low? Statistics like these draw into sharp doubt the validity of the psychological reports expressing a causal relationship between violent video games and violent children.

Patrick R. Byrd,
"It's All Fun and Games Until Someone Gets Hurt!
The Effectiveness of Proposed Video Game
Legislation on Reducing Violence in Children,"
Houston Law Review, *Summer 2007.*

gust 2005 found a clear causal link between violent games and teen aggression." But as political watchdog site GamePolitics.com astutely reported, Dr. Elizabeth Carll, who co-chaired the study, wanted to make clear the "the resolution did not state that there was a direct causal link to an increase in teen violence as a result of playing videogames. Rather, [it stated] an increase in aggressive behavior, aggressive thoughts, angry feelings, and a decrease in helpful behavior as a result of playing violent videogames."

If no one has said there's a causal link between games and real-life violence, why does it keep making headlines, and why do these studies get cited so much? "The [American Psychological Association] is a political organization . . . and they do what is politically expedient like any other group," says Dr. Christopher J. Ferguson of Texas A&M International University's Department of Behavioral, Applied Sciences and Criminal Justice. Ferguson recently released a study named, with typically academic wordiness, "Evidence for publication bias in videogame violence effects literature: A meta-analytic review." In it, he finds what he calls "a systematic bias for hot-button issues" that results in over-statements and misleading results.

The authors of the reports bristle when their research is challenged. Dill, after agreeing to be interviewed for this story, later e-mailed to request that her interview not be used because of what she perceived to be an effort to "push the tired 'party line' that the research is wrong." Her colleague, Anderson, declined entirely, saying an interview would be "pointless."

But it's not just their research that's being challenged—it's the manner in which the findings are presented. "From the present body of literature, there's nothing that supports a relationship between violent videogame playing and aggression—not correlational or causal," Ferguson says. "The moral of the story is that scientists ought to be using much more measured tones in discussing what has become a political issue rather than giving in to the urge to engage in hyperbole." In other words, violent games sell—not to kids, but to the general public at large. Like Elvis in the 50s, or *Dungeons & Dragons* in the 1980s, videogames are still viewed as the dangerous scourge of youth culture. In the face of awful, inexplicable tragedies, media violence is an easy target.

Context Is Important

What's lost to the game-violence critics and public is a dose of reality, not only about the truth of the results but the context.

"I don't think they understand the way the media are used in daily life enough," Williams says of the researchers. "They tend to focus more on lab research and ignore long-term research. People in the psychology community are less likely to pay attention to the social context of media use." But others are. The British Board of Film Classification conducted a survey that found that "the violence helps make the play exhilaratingly out of reach of ordinary life. . . . Gamers seem not to lose awareness that they are playing a game and do not mistake the game for real life."

And considered in light of recent youth crime statistics, all the noise blasts don't pass the muster of common sense. In 2005, for example, just 12 percent of the videogames sold were violent enough to bear an M-rating [mature] by the Entertainment Software Ratings Board, the industry's voluntary ratings group. At the same time, youth crime is dropping precipitously. The number of kids under 17 who committed murder fell 65 percent between 1993 and 2004. "If this was affecting all kids in a bad way we'd see something," argues Dr. Cheryl Olson, professor of psychiatry at the Harvard Medical School's Center for Mental Health and Media.

Even the surgeon general's youth-violence report, which the FCC cites in its recent findings, couldn't find a convincing link. "Taken together, findings to date suggest that media violence has a relatively small impact on violence," the surgeon general reported. And the specific inferences about game violence were even less swaying. "The overall effect size for both randomized and correlational studies was small for physical aggression and moderate for aggressive thinking . . . ," the surgeon general found. "The impact of videogames on violent behavior has yet to be determined."

So what are we left with? A possible link between violent media and loosely defined "aggressive behavior" (noise blasts, clown-doll punching, and so on) but no evidence that playing violent games actually causes violent—let alone criminal—

actions in real life. "It's time to move beyond blanket condemnations and frightening anecdotes and focus on developing targeted educational and policy interventions based on solid data," Olson suggested. "As with the entertainment of earlier generations, we may look back on today's games with nostalgia, and our grandchildren may wonder what the fuss was about."

| *"Today's young people are being trained
to wage war by playing video games."*

Video Games Should Not
Teach War

Dan Costa

In the following viewpoint, Dan Costa puts forth his view that video games should not be used to teach war. As an example, he talks about Special Force 2, *a game created by a Lebanese paramilitary group called Hezbollah. The game is based on a war between the Lebanese and Israelis that took place in 2006. He describes the game as "blatant propaganda for reaching a new generation of militants." He also discusses* America's Army, *a game produced by the American military, and games produced by Kuma Reality, all of which stem from real events. Costa contends that although he likes first-person shooter games, they should not be based on actual wars. Costa is the editor of consumer electronics* PC Magazine.

As you read, consider the following questions:

1. According to the author, what are the American public's two responses to *Special Force 2?*

2. According to the author, how many registered users does *America's Army* have?

3. What does Costa say is in bad taste?

Orson Scott Card's sci-fi classic *Ender's Game* is practically required reading for high-school students these days, and that's probably a good thing. Just like the book's Ender Wiggan, today's young people are being trained to wage war by playing video games.

This past summer [2007] Hezbollah, the Lebanese-based Islamist paramilitary group, released *Special Force 2*, a first-person shooter based on its pointless 34-day war with Israel in 2006. In the game, players are asked to destroy Israeli tanks and launch Katyusha rockets at Israeli towns. Hezbollah even held a launch party in Beirut for the game's release, decorated with disabled tanks and Israeli helmets captured during the conflict.

Hezbollah has gone to great lengths to declare the war a victory for its side. Most estimates put the death toll at 158 Israelis, mainly soldiers. More than 1,200 people, mostly civilians, were killed in Lebanon.

But that is in the real world. In the game, the more Israeli soldiers you kill, the more weapons and points you get. And whoever gets the most points wins. Evidently, *Ender's Game* has been translated into Arabic.

Militant Propaganda

If this sounds like a blatant propaganda tool for reaching a new generation of potential militants, it is. And a statement from Hezbollah's media official makes the game's purpose clear. Oh yes, Hezbollah has a media official. In fact, it has an entire Internet division dedicated to getting its message out to the world and attracting supporters. The official, Sheikh Ali Daher, said, "This game presents the culture of the resistance to children: that occupation must be resisted and that land and the nation must be guarded."

Games Are Fun, War Isn't

Video games can't—or can't yet—convey the human cost of combat. They pass along the adrenaline rush, the thrill of the fight, and leave out the rest. Games are supposed to be fun, but war isn't. "The violence, the combat—we recognize that's the part of the game people want to play," says Major Chris Chambers, deputy director of the *America's Army* development team. "We treat it openly and honestly. We have a death animation. We don't sugarcoat it. It's real—" He stops and corrects himself. "It's not real; it's simulated. But, we're simulating reality." But it has to be fun too, right? "Bottom line, it's gotta be fun," Chambers agrees. "If it's not fun, you don't have a game."

Lev Grossman, "The Army's Killer App,"
Time, February 28, 2005.

The news coverage about *Special Force 2* elicits two responses from the American public. The first is something like, "Wow, they can make video games over there?" To which the answer is clearly yes. In fact, they've been doing it for years. (The original *Special Force* came out in 2003, but no one cared because the graphics were hopelessly unrealistic, even for jihadists.) The second response is, "Whoa, what kind of morally bankrupt society would produce such a product and then sell it to kids?" To which the answer is: a society a lot like ours.

Let me confess here and now, I really like first-person shooters. I remember acquiring a prerelease copy of *Doom* on floppy disk in 1993, rushing back to my PC, and then blasting away at demons well into the night. I may have lost a step or two since then—I don't tend to last too long in online *Halo* tournaments—but I can still kill hours playing *Medal of Honor* or *Resistance: Fall of Man*. Even so, there comes a time when we should take a hard look at the implicit—and explicit—messages in the games we play.

America's Popular Propaganda

Besides, it isn't as if we didn't beat Hezbollah to the video-game-as-recruitment-tool party. U.S. taxpayers paid for the development of the U.S. Army's official game, *America's Army [AA]*, a tactical multiplayer first-person shooter. Since it launched in 2002, *AA* has been downloaded 40 million times, and it now has more than 8.5 million registered users. An Xbox version is launching this fall [2007]. Knowing it is under the microscope, the developers of *America's Army* avoid re-creating specific real-life battles—don't expect to see the Battle for Tora Bora anytime soon. But although the Army takes pains to talk up the team-oriented, values-driven nature of the game, there is still a fair amount of running and gunning. For what it's worth, *America's Army* kills *Special Force 2* when it comes to pure polygons-per-second graphics power.

Of course, the private sector, too, wants to profit from virtual warfare. Kuma Reality Games specializes in re-creating real-world battles drawn from recent news events. The company often uses stories from soldiers and satellite maps handed over by the U.S. military to build its scenarios. From the infamous "last stand" in Mosul of Saddam Hussein's sons Uday and Qusay to a brutal assault on a Baghdad police station that left 17 Iraq officers dead, the game is ultrarealistic. Kuma's Web site urges readers: "Stop watching the news and get in the game!"

Maybe this phenomenon isn't very different from re-creating Omaha Beach in *Medal of Honor*, or *Law & Order*'s "ripped from the headlines" formula for its weekly episodes. Maybe it is just following too closely on the heels of the events, or is too real, or too unreal. Or maybe it is just in extremely bad taste. We are playing games on virtual battlefields before the blood has dried on the real ones.

Kuma's perspective is pretty straightforward, and its tagline doesn't do anything to obscure it. "In a world being torn apart by international conflict, one thing is on everyone's mind as they finish watching the nightly news: 'Man, this would make a great game.'"

Maybe, but that isn't a game I want to play.

> "With 6 million registered users, the PC
> [personal computer] game has attracted
> new soldiers to the ranks; 20 percent of
> the starting class at West Point had
> played America's Army prior to ma-
> triculating, and 20 to 40 percent of re-
> cruited soldiers had as well."

Video Games Are Good Training Tools for the Military

Grace Jean

In the following viewpoint, Grace Jean describes the use of a video game, America's Army, as a training and recruitment tool for the military. Jean describes new adaptations that expand the personal computer game to include real simulations. She quotes military personnel, who say that the game has improved the performance of young recruits and has increased recruitment numbers. Jean is the senior editor of National Defense Magazine.

As you read, consider the following questions:

1. According to the author, what was the original mission of *America's Army*?

Grace Jean, "America's Army: Game Branches Out into Real Combat Training," *National Defense*, February 2006, pp. 34–36. Copyright 2006 National Defense Industrial Association. Reproduced by permission.

2. According to Christopher Chambers, as quoted by the author, what factor in games keeps the participant engaged?

3. According to the author, how does the cost of maintaining America's Army.com compare to the cost of maintaining GoArmy.com?

When the Army launched its PC-based video game, *America's Army* [in 2002] the service's intention was to connect with young people, encourage teamwork and promote its core values. But now the action game is morphing beyond its original mission, becoming the platform for numerous other military and government training simulations.

"Before we even launched the public game, we knew from development that this type of technology was pretty powerful for training, especially small units–small infantry teams, special forces teams," said Christopher Chambers, deputy director for *America's Army*, in an interview with *National Defense*.

The game's technology has been incorporated into a number of virtual training applications already, including embedded trainers, in which *America's Army* software runs on the computers that drive their respective weapons systems, such as the Bradley, the Javelin and the CROWS, or common remotely operated weapons station.

At the Serious Games Summit in Arlington, [Virginia], Michael Bode, a software engineer for the Army's Redstone Arsenal, demonstrated the prototype of a Tube-launched, Optically-tracked, Wire-guided (TOW) anti-tank missile system trainer—one of the newest simulations that was built with *America's Army* software.

"We're turning it around incredibly fast because of the high re-use factor" of *America's Army*, he said.

But the game's applications stretch beyond individual weapons training.

"What we can do is connect our visualization to real lessons, real vehicles and other simulations, and now we have a more complete set of training levels, from the team up to the division," said Chambers.

The project's next goal is to leverage the service's simulation centers, which utilize computer technologies to prepare soldiers for battlefield scenarios.

Video Games Allow for Complex Training Operations

By linking up the individual game-based virtual trainers with large-scale training operations, the Army can have multi-level tiers of virtual training going on, he said.

"The training need that we can service well is the live, multi-player interactions in a distributed fashion," said Chambers. For example, the game could assist the training for National Guard units, which are scattered across a state and throughout the country. "The *America's Army* product is designed, by its nature, to be Internet-capable and very easy to connect to across the country or around the world. So that allows us to do distributed training and secret training" without having to bring everyone together in one place, he said.

At the games summit, Jerry Hleiter, of Anteon Corp., gave a demonstration of how the technology is being incorporated into the Army's simulation centers via a 360-degree immersive environment.

"The environment becomes the training medium, and that's where *America's Army* plays in," he said. "We use *America's Army* as the visual system."

Inside such a simulation, soldiers can train on foot or in mock-ups of vehicles and aircraft. They wear vests with audio systems embedded in them that send our signals to the simulation's location system, enabling a virtual player to interact with the live player and vice versa.

Computerized War Games

The Army Operations Research Office at Maryland's Johns Hopkins University developed the first truly computerized war games. Beginning with *Air Defense Simulation* in 1948 and the *Carmonette* series of simulations in 1953, these systems eliminated much of the manual work of moving pieces, rolling dice, looking up results in a table and calculating final results, [Roger] Smith [the Army's Program Executive Office for Simulation, Training, and Instrumentation] said.

"The players could focus on the tactical movement and leave the complexity of manipulation to the computer," he said. . . .

In today's personal-gaming age, Smith said entertainment games and technologies are being modified and used in the military domain, and traditional military games have been re-tooled for casual gamers and sold for entertainment.

Carrie McLeroy, "History of Military Gaming,"
Soldiers of Fortune, *September 2008.*

"By leveraging game technology and having that feedback, we can have consequence to an action," said Hleiter.

In a convoy trainer simulation demonstration in which six vehicles are tasked with hunting down a bomb maker, the first vehicle, controlled by a live player sitting at a desktop computer, is engaged by snipers firing from a building. The second vehicle, manned by four live soldiers riding in a Humvee mock-up inside the simulation center, provides supporting cover.

The game technology also enables limitless replaying possibilities, which is beneficial in training, said Chambers.

"You could run through virtually the same environment multiple times, and multiple things happen that create that decision-making [process] that makes it a more robust training system," he said.

America's Army is working on ways to recall the data of a game for after-action reviews and other training applications, he added.

With video game technology proliferating, the impact of playing those games has come under scrutiny by institutions, including the University of Rochester and the Army Research Institute.

The Impact of Games on Training

"Both of them concluded that gaming, and in particular, a first-person action game, like *America's Army*, or its counterpart, does have an effect on training," said Chambers.

The University of Rochester study found that 10 hours of playing a video game could have a significant impact on visual acuity. The Army Research Institute study discovered that procedural information is retained at a 12 percent higher rate than factual information in the same game.

"Games are designed with an entertainment focus, so by their very design, they engage the participant and keep him engaged, as opposed to the design process that brought the traditional military simulation where the fun factor, the engagement factor, wasn't a paramount factor," said Chambers.

Making simulations more fun not only can help train better soldiers but it also can help in the recruiting cycle, he said.

With 6 million registered users, the PC game has attracted new soldiers to the ranks; 20 percent of the starting class at West Point had played *America's Army* prior to matriculating, and 20 to 40 percent of recruited soldiers had as well, said Col. Casey Wardynski, director of *America's Army*.

"America's Army.com gets 60,000 hits per day. That's more than GoArmy.com. It's one of the major referrers to GoArmy-.com," he said.

The America's Army.com Web site costs $4,000 a year to maintain. By comparison, GoArmy.com costs the Army about $8 million a year, he added.

"A kid comes to us, believes in *America's Army* and he sees *America's Army*, the visualization for all of these training devices. We've got a leap forward in terms of his confidence, and also he or she is more likely to be able to play it, because they're familiar with the key conventions," said Chambers.

Some of the pre-basic combat training will include *America's Army* simulations, such as the future soldier trainer and the future soldier training system.

[In February 2006], the team will upgrade the public version's game engine from Epic Games' Unreal Engine 2 to Unreal Engine 3.

America's Army also is reaching more young players with its recent expansion into video game consoles. Next month, [March 2006] San Francisco-based Ubisoft plans to release *"America's Army: Rise of a Soldier"*—a game based on the original PC version—on Sony's PlayStation 2.

Chambers said the new games could help extend the soldiers' training day if consoles and other cheaper devices were placed in the barracks. He also said the team is working on cell phone games and other wireless applications.

"We don't see *America's Army* as the answer for every level of training," he said. But the game's visualization, high-quality graphics and the multi-player Internet-connected playing can help in improving many of the government's training devices, he added.

"I think it is great if our biggest concern is that children are playing shoot-'em-ups. A couple of thousand years ago, families went to the Colosseum in Rome to cheer as gladiators sliced their opponents' limbs or were eaten by lions."

Violence in Video Games Reduces Violence in the Real World

Charles Herold

Charles Herold is a video game critic for the New York Times. *In the following viewpoint, he asserts that video game violence is cathartic and reduces violence in the real world. He describes three video games to illustrate his point. Herold believes that the violence children enjoy in video games is harmless compared to real-life violent entertainment such as boxing.*

As you read, consider the following questions:

1. What threats to today's children does Herold suggest have been superseded by video game violence in the opinion of video game critics?

2. What does the author say about studies of aggressiveness in children?

3. How does the author compare video game violence to a boxing match?

In the minds of some, video game violence has superseded television violence and satanic rock lyrics as the No. 1 threat to today's children. It is video games, rather than easy access to guns, the glorification of war or a culture that uses violence as the first resort to resolve conflict that makes us savages, or so I am informed in the occasional angry e-mail message from a reader after I write about a particularly violent video game.

I could argue the point. I could mention the theory that video game violence is cathartic, that it has led to a decrease in violence among youngsters. I could suggest that studies showing a short-term rise in aggressiveness in children after they play video games are meaningless if there is no comparable study on short-term aggressiveness after they play football.

I won't, because I think it is great if our biggest concern is that children are playing shoot-'em-ups. A couple of thousand years ago, families went to the Colosseum in Rome to cheer as gladiators sliced their opponents' limbs or were eaten by lions. Now, the closest one can get to that experience is playing Capcom's *Shadow of Rome*.

Game Violence Doesn't Compare to the Real Thing

The game takes place immediately after the assassination of Julius Caesar, and revolves around the efforts of two friends,

Agrippa and Octavianus, to save the man who has been framed for his murder. *Shadow of Rome* is actually two games that share a single plot: powerful Agrippa is the star of a brutal and exciting fighting game, while the wimpy and more studious Octavianus must reach his goals through stealth. There are some chariot races, although these are simply a diversion from the main game branches.

Agrippa's game is one of constant, brutal fighting, first on the battlefield and later in gladiatorial events. In the ring, Agrippa will face giants, other gladiators and the occasional tiger. He is armed with a variety of weapons, including a mace for bashing, a spear that can be swung to injure multiple foes and a scimitar that slices off limbs.

Weapons shatter within minutes, and while you can often retrieve swords from vanquished opponents or steal them from living ones, the most powerful weapons are supplied by the cheering throng. The crowd is happiest when you pull off especially brutal moves with names like meat sculpture and juicy tomato. And if you steal a weapon, slice off someone's arm or knock an opponent into the air, the crowd will shower you with rose petals and throw huge, lethal weapons to you. This can backfire; your opponents will often grab these weapons first.

As Agrippa battles, Octavianus spies on senators he suspects were involved in Caesar's murder. Unskilled in weaponry, Octavianus relies on stealth and cunning, hiding in large pots, knocking out guards from behind with a handy vase or stealing clothes and passing himself off as a senator or even a maid. You must choose your replies wisely if stopped and questioned by suspicious guards. *Shadow of Rome*'s approach is sometimes goofily over the top. Some of Agrippa's weapons are as big as he is. Octavianus can knock guards unconscious by dropping a banana peel in their path. He uses frogs to scare away women.

Shadow of Rome's gameplay glistens, but its presentation is somewhat lackluster. Graphics are well animated but a little drab. The tedious story plays out like one of those 1950's Roman epics starring Victor Mature, and contains such clichés as a mysterious beautiful woman and a sadistic villain who says things like, "I'll make him pay." After killing a vanquished opponent at the crowd's behest, Agrippa yells: "Are you satisfied? Is it really enjoyable to see men kill each other like animals?" It's as if he expects the people in the crowd to hang their heads in shame and file quietly out of the Colosseum.

One can understand Agrippa's distress. There is something morbid about watching other people battle. At the same time, doing it yourself can be extremely painful.

Harmless Fighting Games

Video games exist for those who want to fight ferociously without getting hurt. *Tekken 5*, Namco's exciting martial arts game, generally satisfies this desire, although all the mad pounding on your game controller can make your fingers sore.

Tekken is straight one-on-one fighting. Two opponents punch, kick and throw each other with such force that the ground ruptures as they fall. Each fighter has some unique moves. I especially liked Christie for her gymnastics-style fighting and ridiculously skimpy outfit. Actions are beautifully animated, and it is thrilling when you manage to throw your opponents straight up in the air and keep them there with a series of well-placed kicks.

Punching and kicking is straightforward and intuitive with use of the left analog stick to determine whether to hit high or low and one button for each arm and leg. More elaborate rolls and jumps come out of reasonably logical button combinations. Only the flashiest moves require the pure button-sequence memorization always found in martial arts games;

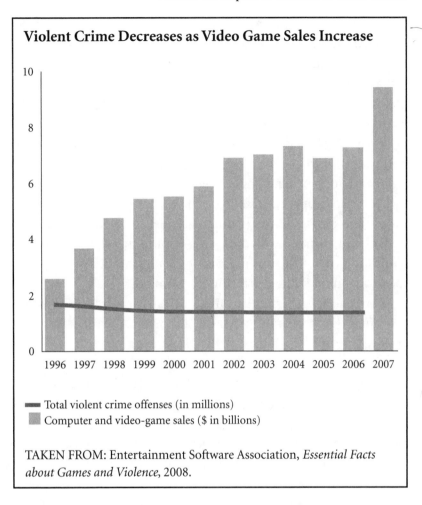

Violent Crime Decreases as Video Game Sales Increase

- ━ Total violent crime offenses (in millions)
- ▨ Computer and video-game sales ($ in billions)

TAKEN FROM: Entertainment Software Association, *Essential Facts about Games and Violence*, 2008.

there is no simple and intuitive way to express complex moves like turning hand over hand using your legs as a propeller.

This bloodless savagery takes place in a number of beautiful arenas, including a moonlit field of large white flowers and an ice field complete with a penguin audience.

Boxing

Those seeking a less fanciful fighting experience can turn to *Fight Night Round 2*, an impressive boxing game from Electronic Arts.

Boxing is sometimes called the sweet science, but I have always thought of it as two thugs pounding each other. *Fight Night* puts the lie to that notion; playing the game requires fast reflexes and cunning. You must anticipate your player's moves as you duck and parry, waiting for an opportunity to lay in a well-timed punch.

Fight *Night*'s ingenious control scheme lets you control both arms with the right analog stick. Push the stick to the right and your boxer punches right. Push left and up and he'll throw a left uppercut. Hold down a trigger button and you can dodge blows. There is a natural feel to movement as you dodge and punch or rattle your opponent with a series of blinding blows. Controls are easy to understand, but the intricacies of boxing take much longer to master.

Playing *Fight Night* gives me a certain admiration for boxers, but doesn't change my utter abhorrence for a sport that revolves around trying to inflict severe damage on a fellow human.

I suggest that those concerned with video game violence attend a boxing match and watch people cheer as a man is hammered to the floor, then watch children sitting on a couch, pushing buttons as animated gladiators die on-screen.

Perhaps then people will realize that an animated spear is better than a real fist and they will e-mail me with their gratitude for luring the world away from true violence. They are most welcome.

"When a man or woman picks up a weapon and premeditates the end of another human life, it is . . . because that individual made a conscious choice—not to play a game, but to kill."

Video Games Are Not Responsible for People's Violent Actions

Christopher J. Ferguson

In the following viewpoint, Christopher J. Ferguson argues that video games should not be blamed for violence and that this blame arises from the need to find reassurance after devastating acts of violence. He contends that various media such as books, music, television, and movies have been held as scapegoats for personal failings, which he says are the real cause of violence. Ferguson is an assistant professor at Texas A&M University.

As you read, consider the following questions:

1. Explain what Ferguson means when he says people linking video games to crime are using a high-base-rate behavior to explain a low-base-rate behavior.

2. What did the author's analysis conclude about video games and aggressive behavior?

3. What example does the author give to support his assertion that violent games can increase performance in some areas of cognition?

In the wake of the Virginia Tech shootings [in 2007], it was distressing to see the paroxysms of neurotic finger-pointing and "expert witnessing" that inevitably followed. Beyond noting simply that a bad (evil, some would say) man chose one day to make the lives of other individuals as hellish as he felt his own to be, I don't think we'll ever come up with much more of a scientific explanation for what leads people, mostly men, to become mass murderers. Let me put that another way: Beyond individuals who actually threaten in advance to carry out school shootings (which a recent Secret Service report concluded was the only really useful indicator), no other behavior is particularly predictive of such acts of senseless violence.

That's not very satisfying, is it? Perhaps for that reason, it seems to me that increasingly, as a culture, we have shied away from holding people responsible for their behaviors, and instead prefer to seek out easy or even abstract entities to blame. Events like school shootings tend to make people nervous. Nervous people like reassurance. We would like to think that such events can be explained, predicted, and prevented. We like scientists and politicians who stand up and claim to have the answers so that we can fix the problem.

Placing Blame on the Media

The difficulty is that this often leads to a witch hunt or moral panic, wherein explanations rely on weak social science or what is politically expedient. In past centuries, a variety of art forms have taken the blame for society's problems. From literature to religious texts, to jazz, rock 'n' roll, and rap, to television, movies, and comic books, people have viewed various media as being responsible for personal failings, as if such media were like the serpent in the Garden of Eden, leading us astray from our natural goodness. Increasingly, in the past two decades, video games have been the scapegoat du jour. The video-game platform is the newest kid on the media block and, as such, is subject to a particularly high dose of suspicion and scrutiny. I think that this is wrong and, indeed, dangerous.

It seemed that the Virginia Tech rampage was barely over before a few pundits began speculating on the role of video games. The lawyer and activist Jack Thompson asserted that violent games such as *Counter-Strike* may have been responsible for the shooter's actions. Although I have heard little to indicate conclusively that the perpetrator was an avid gamer, the prevalence of game playing among young men makes it likely that he would have crossed paths with a violent game at some point ("He played *Spy Versus Spy* once when he was 12, that's the culprit!"). For instance, a 1996 study found that 98.7 percent of children of either gender played some video games, with violent games, like *Streetfighter II*, particularly popular among young men (93 percent of whom had played that one game alone). Since most young men today play violent video games, it is usually not hard to "link" a violent crime with video-game playing if you are so inclined. This is the classic error of using a high-base-rate (very common) behavior to explain a low-base-rate (rare) behavior. Using video-game-playing habits to predict school shootings is about as useful as noting that most or all school shooters were in the habit of wearing sneakers and concluding that sneakers must be responsible for such violence.

Study Results Are Weak

I actually do research on violent video games. I certainly don't speak for others in the field, some of whom I know will dis-

Video Games Don't Make People Violent

The idea that video games and explicit media content are a threat to society is demonstrably false. Whatever evidence there might be that violent media content causes violent behavior, or that graphic sexual content stimulates unhealthy sexual behavior, there is a simple test that invariably proves otherwise. Buy the game and then take some time to play it over the next few days or weeks—however long you feel is necessary for a proper test. . . .

After you're done, ask yourself a few straightforward questions: Do you want to go outside and steal a car? Do you feel the need to obtain a missile launcher? Do you feel like having sex with a stripper? Or, to more accurately represent the sort of reasoning involved in media-effects claims, do you feel that having sex with a stripper is now a real possibility for you?

Bill Blake, "Go Ahead, Steal My Car,"
Chronicle of Higher Education, *June 27, 2008.*

agree with my perspective, but I do speak from a familiarity with the research and the literature. One meta-analysis of video-game studies, conducted this year [in 2007] by John Sherry, of Michigan State University, found little support for the belief that playing violent games causes aggression. Recently I completed my own meta-analytic review (published in the journal *Aggression and Violent Behavior*) of 25 violent-game studies and found that publication bias and the use of poor and unstandardized measures of aggression were significant problems for this area of research.

My meta-analysis concluded that there was no evidence to support either a causal or correlational relationship between video games and aggressive behavior. My impression is that social science made up its mind that video games cause aggression before many data were available, and has subsequently attempted to fit square pieces of evidence into round theoretical holes. The threshold for what appears to constitute "evidence" is remarkably low. Admittedly, publication bias (the tendency to publish articles that support a hypothesis and not publish those that don't) is very likely a widespread problem in the social sciences and is not unique to video-game studies. Perhaps this is really a reflection on human nature. I may sound hopelessly postmodern here, but sometimes we forget that scientists are mere humans, and that the process of science, as a human enterprise, may always have difficulty rising above a collective and dogmatic pat on the back rather than a meaningful search for truth.

Unfortunately, I think it is a worrisome reflection on social science in general that social scientists may be too prone to make big and frightening pronouncements from weak results. That violent crime rates in the United States have gone down significantly since 1994 (despite some small recent increases) while video games have gotten more popular and more violent should, in and of itself, be sufficient to reject the video-game-violence hypothesis (and the rest of the media-violence hypothesis with it). Some media researchers attempt to defuse this argument by suggesting that "other factors" are at play, but no theory should be allowed to survive such a retreat to an unfalsifiable position—that it never need actually fit with real-world data. Could you imagine how far the debate on global warming would have gotten if the earth's atmospheric temperatures were decreasing while pollutants were being released?

Double Standards for Media Violence

In my opinion, the video-game hypothesis remains because it fits well with the dogma of social science (which has yet to escape from an obsession with deterministic learning models that view humans as passive programmed machines rather than active in determining their own behavior), and it is politically expedient. Politicians can use "media violence" to enact popular (but unconstitutional) legislation censoring or otherwise limiting access to violent media, legislation that can appeal to both political conservatives and political liberals. (Religious conservatives might be bemused to know that some media-violence researchers recently published an article suggesting that reading passages from the Bible with violent content increases "aggression" in much the same way that video games supposedly do. So if video games have to be restricted from children, apparently so do at least some portions of the Bible.) By stating that such legislation is based on "concern for children," politicians can cast their opponents as being unconcerned with children while stripping parents of their rights to decide what media are appropriate for their children. In such a political environment, the video-game-violence hypothesis has persisted long after it should have been laid to rest.

All this is no idle concern. Media issues serve to distract us from more-sensitive topics that may be real contributors to violent behavior, notably violence in families although in fairness, not all abused people become violent offenders. I also posit that many of us prefer to blame others, particularly an abstract entity such as the media, for our problems rather than accept personal responsibility when we or our children behave badly. That's the crux of it, I think. Video games, like the rest of the media, form a faceless specter that we have called into being with our own internal desires for sex and violence, yet can turn against when we need a straw man to blame for our own recklessness.

What's lost in the discussion is that there have been several publications suggesting that violent games may be related to increased performance in some areas of cognition, particularly visuospatial cognition. This is a new research area, and I certainly don't wish to reverse the error of overstating the link between video games and aggression by producing my own overstatement. But I do think that, instead of fueling up the bonfires and throwing in the game consoles, we need to have a serious discussion of both sets of potential effects. Given the allure of violent video games, it may be advisable to consider how some games with violent content may be used to further educational purposes. For instance, a first-person-shooter game (though certainly a mild one compared with some) called *Re-Mission* is being studied in relation to young adults with cancer. One group of youths who played this game demonstrated better cancer-treatment adherence, better self-efficacy and quality of life, and more cancer-related knowledge than did those in a control group who did not play the game. Of course, once the dust settles, it may really be that video games, like most other forms of entertainment, are simply that: entertainment, neither helpful nor harmful.

I don't know how it came to be that we, as a culture, ceased holding people responsible for their actions. How did we come to feel that we are programmed like machines? How did we come to embrace the Brave New World not as a dystopia to be feared but as a panacea for all of our human guilt? When a man or woman picks up a weapon and premeditates the end of another human life, it is not because he or she was programmed by a video game but because that individual made a conscious choice—not to play a game, but to kill. This darkness lurks not within our computers, televisions, books, or music, but rather within our species and, sometimes, ourselves.

Periodical Bibliography

The following articles have been selected to supplement the diverse views presented in this chapter.

Christopher P. Barlett, Richard J. Harris, and Ross Baldassaro
"The Longer You Play, the More Hostile You Feel: Examination of First Person Shooter Video Games and Aggression During Video Game Play," *Aggressive Behavior*, November–December 2007.

Marije Nije Bijvank
"Violent Video Game Effects on Children and Adolescents: Theory, Research, and Public Policy," *Child and Adolescent Mental Health*, May 2008.

Elizabeth K. Carll
"Violent Video Games: Rehearsing Aggression," *Chronicle of Higher Education*, July 13, 2007.

Robert Coffey
"Blamestorming: Games Aren't Evil, but Tyne Daly Is," *Computer Gaming World*, December 2003.

Joel E. Collier, Pearson Liddell Jr., and Gloria J. Liddell
"Exposure of Violent Video Games to Children and Public Policy Implications," *Journal of Public Policy & Marketing*, Spring 2008.

Christopher Dean
"Returning the Pig to Its Pen: A Pragmatic Approach to Regulating Minors' Access to Violent Video Games," *George Washington Law Review*, November 2006.

J.C. Herz and Michael R. Macedonia
"Computer Games and the Military: Two Views," *Defense Horizons*, April 2002.

Paul Kearney and Maja Pivec
"Sex, Lies and Video Games," *British Journal of Educational Technology*, 2007.

Stacy L. Wood
"Consuming Violence," *Business & Economic Review*, July–September 2007.

OPPOSING
VIEWPOINTS®
SERIES

CHAPTER 4

How Should Video Games Be Regulated?

Chapter Preface

The potential negative influences of video games, especially on young people, has been a cause for controversy since 1976, when a game called *Death Race*, which centered on driving a car to run over "gremlins," was released. The controversy became particularly intense in 2004, when the game *Grand Theft Auto: San Andreas* was released by Rockstar Games. At first, it appeared to be just another in a series of games in which the player takes on the role of a criminal in a big city. Later, a modification by users revealed a hidden mini-game in which the main character has sexual intercourse with a female character. This scene became known as the "hot coffee" mod, or modification, and became a focal point for opponents of sex and violence in video games.

Former senator Hillary Rodham Clinton has been a prominent leader in the movement against video games such as *Grand Theft Auto*, which feature criminals as the main characters and graphically depict sex and violence. Clinton was instrumental in introducing a bill recommending legislation that would govern video game ratings and sales. She challenged the Federal Trade Commission to launch an investigation into the hot coffee mod to determine whether Rockstar Games should be held responsible and to reconsider the game's "M" (mature) rating.

The viewpoints in the following chapter include a variety of perspectives on the issue of regulation of video games. Some, such as Clinton, believe that legislation is necessary. Others think that the game industry, in particular the Entertainment Software Ratings Board, the game creators, and the retailers, should be responsible for regulation. Still others expect parents to be involved in choosing the games their children play, with guidance from the game industry. Some observers criticize both the current rating system and potential regulating legislation, believing neither is useful.

> *"We should all be deeply disturbed that a game which now permits the simulation of lewd sexual acts in an interactive format with highly realistic graphics has fallen into the hands of young people across the country."*

Legislation Should Regulate Video Game Use

Senator Hillary Rodham Clinton

Former senator Hillary Rodham Clinton has been an advocate for legislation that regulates video game sales. Along with Senators Joseph Lieberman (D–Connecticut) and Evan Bayh (D–Indiana), she sponsored the bill known as the Family Entertainment Protection Act, introduced in the Senate in 2005. That bill was subsequently referred to the Committee on Commerce, Science, and Transportation. The following viewpoint explains her argument that a particular game, Grand Theft Auto: San Andreas, *should receive an Adults Only rating rather than a Mature rating, following reports that pornographic and violent content can be unlocked in the game by following instructions readily available on the Internet.*

The Office of Senator Hillary Rodham Clinton, "Senator Clinton Announces Legislation to Keep Inappropriate Video Games Out of the Hands of Children," July 14, 2005.

As you read, consider the following questions:

1. According to a National Institute on Media and the Family study quoted in this viewpoint, what percentage of boys between the ages of 7 and 14 purchased and played M-rated games?

2. According to the National Institute study, what percentage of retailers train their employees to use the rating system?

3. In addition to investigating *Grand Theft Auto: San Andreas*, what does Clinton ask the Federal Trade Commission to examine?

Senator Hillary Rodham Clinton today [July 14, 2005] announced that she will introduce legislation to help keep inappropriate video games out of the hands of children. She also called upon the Federal Trade Commission (FTC) to take immediate action to determine the source of graphic pornographic and violent content appearing on the *Grand Theft Auto: San Andreas* video game. Recent reports have revealed that this graphic content can be unlocked by following instructions widely available on the Internet.

"The disturbing material in *Grand Theft Auto* and other games like it is stealing the innocence of our children and it's making the difficult job of being a parent even harder," said Senator Clinton. "I am announcing these measures today because I believe that the ability of our children to access pornographic and outrageously violent material on video games rated for adults is spiraling out of control."

Senator Clinton announced that the legislation she will introduce will put some teeth into video game ratings by instituting a financial penalty for retailers who fail to enforce the rules. It will prohibit the sale of violent and sexually explicit video games to minors and put in place a $5000 penalty for those who violate the law.

Recent research has confirmed links between exposure to violent video games and aggressive behavior in children and a groundbreaking new study by researchers at Indiana University School of Medicine show that playing violent video games triggers unusual brain activity among aggressive adolescents with disruptive behavior disorders. Senator Clinton noted that this is just the latest piece of evidence that confirms the potentially damaging impact of these games on children. Senator Clinton also noted that the current, industry enforced system is not yet working as it should and is not acting as a deterrent to kids accessing inappropriate video games, underscoring the need for today's action.

In calling for the FTC to launch an investigation, Senator Clinton urged the FTC to determine whether an Adults Only (AO) rating is more appropriate than the current Mature (M) rating for the *Grand Theft Auto: San Andreas* video game given this new, alarming content. She also requested that the FTC examine the adequacy of retailers' rating enforcement policies.

According to research by the National Institute on Media and the Family, games rated M, which means they are appropriate only for people aged 17 or older, are relatively easy for teenagers and even children as young as age 7 to obtain. In the National Institute's recent study, 50 percent of boys between the ages of 7 and 14 successfully purchased M-rated video games, and an astonishing 87 percent of boys play M-rated games. Furthermore, nearly a quarter of retailers in the study don't even understand the ratings they are supposed to enforce, and only half of the stores train employees in the use of the ratings.

"No wonder these games are falling into the hands of our children and no wonder so many parents feel every day like they are fighting this battle with their hands tied behind their backs," said Senator Clinton. "We need to do better. We need to do everything we can to make sure that parents have a line

An Excerpt from Proposed Family Entertainment Protection Act

SEC. 4. PROHIBITION ON SALE OF VIOLENT VIDEO GAMES TO MINORS.

(a) In General- No business shall sell or rent, or permit the sale or rental of any video game with a Mature, Adults-Only, or Ratings Pending rating from the Entertainment Software Ratings Board to any individual who has not attained the age of 17 years. . . .

(c)Penalty- The manager or agent of the manager acting in a managerial capacity of a business found to be in violation of the prohibition under subsection (a) shall be subject to a civil penalty, community service, or both not to exceed—

1. (1) $1,000 or 100 hours of community service for the first violation; and

2. (2) $5,000 or 500 hours of community service for each subsequent violation.

Hillary Clinton, Joseph Lieberman, and Evan Bayh,
"Family Entertainment Protection Act," December 16, 2005.

of defense against violent and graphic video games and other content that go against the values they are trying to instill in their children."

Letter to the Federal Trade Commission

The following is the text of Senator Clinton's letter to the FTC:

Recent reports have revealed that the video game, Grand Theft Auto: San Andreas, *has graphic pornographic content* which may be unlocked by following instructions widely available on the Internet. The Entertainment Software Ratings Board (ESRB) has given this game a Mature (M) rating, which means it is appropriate only for people age 17 or older. In all likelihood, this revelation means the game deserves an Adults Only (AO) rating. Alarmingly, it seems that no one yet knows the source of this content. The ESRB is investigating this matter and I am hopeful its investigation will be vigorous and thorough. But the public has a strong interest in learning the answer quickly. We should all be deeply disturbed that a game which now permits the simulation of lewd sexual acts in an interactive format with highly realistic graphics has fallen into the hands of young people across the country. I therefore urge you to take immediate action to determine the source of this content and the appropriateness of the M rating in light of its vast accessibility, and to make your findings public. Parents who rely on the ratings to make decisions to shield their children from influences that they believe could be harmful, should be informed right away if the system is broken. Parents face an uphill battle just understanding the ratings system. They cannot and should not be expected to second guess it.

I also ask that you conduct a careful examination of the adequacy of retailers' rating enforcement policies. According to research conducted by the National Institute on Media and the Family, M games are relatively easy for teenagers and even children as young as 7 to obtain. In the National Institute's recent study, 50% of boys between the ages of 7 and 14 successfully purchased M-rated video games. Furthermore, only 76% of retailers in the study said they understand the ratings they are supposed to enforce. And only half of the stores train employees in the use of the ratings. The National Institute has determined that 87% of boys play M-rated games and 78% list an M-rated game among their favorites. As a Senator, I hear from parents all the time about the frustration they feel as they try to pass their own values onto their children in a world where this type *of material is readily accessible. There is no doubting the fact that the widespread availability of sexually explicit and graphically violent video games makes the challenge of parenting much harder. I will be exploring legislation to help parents with this challenge when it comes to purchasing video games soon and I hope you will work with me to ensure that the ratings system— the best tool parents have to filter this material—is meaningful.*

> "It's time both sides of this dispute, the angry American parents and the aloof games industry, worked together to help change the way games are sold."

Video Game Ratings Should Be Revised for Clarity and Accountability

James Paterson

James Paterson is a 24-year-old from England, who has played video games since he was a child. In the following viewpoint, he describes the British system of rating games, which is based on age, and recommends that the United States adopt a similar system that does not allow adult games to be sold to children, rather than filing lawsuits and staging rallies and protests. Paterson states that with this type of system, parents can decide if they want to purchase games for their children that are above the child's age range, as his parents did for him when they bought Grand Theft Auto *(rated 18) when he was sixteen.*

As you read, consider the following questions:

1. On what point do lawyer Jack Thompson and the author agree?

2. What does Paterson say happened when *Grand Theft Auto: San Andreas* was released in England?

3. How does the author say the ratings should be enforced by retailers?

Hello, my name is James and I'm a gamer. As a 24-year-old male living in a suburb of Manchester, England, I feel safe telling you this. In 2006's Britain, playing games is fine, it's fun and, dare I say it, it's fashionable.

But it wasn't always like this.

I've always been a gamer. I had a Spectrum [early British computer]. I had a Mega Drive [sold in North America as Sega Genesis] and I've had all of Sony's consoles, not forgetting an Xbox or two along the way. But back in 1994 it was all about the Mega Drive. Aged 12 I was very comfortable in the belief that Sonic [the Hedgehog, a video game character] was the best thing since sliced bread—I wore red and white trainers and I even spiked my hair like him.

The problem was that this was not exactly a fashionable thing to do. Exploring Sonic's Green Hill Zone and wandering around Toe Jam and Earl's version of Earth didn't make me stand out as cool—and let's not even talk about the effects of playing with the bears in *Altered Beast*.

Of course I've grown up a bit since then and, it's safe to say, so has gaming. The colourful world of platform games still exists, but it's no longer the driving force behind the worldwide gaming revolution. Instead, it's Rockstar's *Grand Theft Auto* series—it's the blockbusters like *Halo* and now *Gears of War*. Bye bright blue Sonic, hello stealth-like Sam Fisher.

There is one big difference between the games I used to play and the games we play now—they all carry high age ratings. *Splinter Cell* is for over 15s, *Halo* can be yours if your

Critic Jack Thompson Clarifies His Position

Is it fair that certain games should be banned from the whole gaming populace, despite the argument that only a tiny minority of gamers are easily influenced?

No, of course not. In a free society, adults can pretty much get what they want and should. You gamers need to get off the "Jack Thompson wants to ban video games" nonsense. I had a kid in New York call me the other day screaming at me because of that. I said please, listen to my real position. He listened. He was a nice and polite guy. When I was done, he said "Hey, I agree with every-thing you have to say on this. This was very cool." I asked him what prompted him to call. He said, "Our eighth grade social studies class was talking about you, and I thought I would call you." I said, "Tell your teacher I will be happy to address the entire class by speaker phone so they can hear what my real views are as the industry's chief critic," and he said that was very cool. Facts are very, very cool. Caricatures of critics are stupid.

Jack Thompson, "Interview,"
2008. http://play.tm.

date of birth makes you 16 and *Grand Theft Auto*—well, prove you're 18 and the delights of carjacking, mass murder and drug running can be yours.

Well, as long as you live in the UK [United Kingdom] or Europe. In America they do things differently. You won't find games marked '12', '15' and '18' there. Instead, games are tagged with words like 'Teen' and 'Mature'. This, according to recognised statistics, leads to 40% of large retailers selling vio-lent games to lone children, no questions asked.

It's been said before that statistics can prove anything, however if 4 out of 10 young children can get hold of violent videogames, it certainly sounds like there is a problem. That's why a growing number of people in the US are pressing for change.

Of course, they are pressing for change in an entirely American way. Stories of mass protests against videogames, class action lawsuits and various other activities make their way around the world at an alarming pace thanks to the wonders of YouTube and any other number of gaming websites. These often portray those pushing for change in an unfortunate light. Whether it's through question and answer sessions where the interviewers already seem to have preconceived ideas or edited comments not showing the whole picture, it's often hard to identify with Mr and Mrs American Protester. Their signs proclaiming offences against God and calling industry personnel sociopaths don't do much for a liberal public.

I should admit that until very recently I too would have believed that the protesters were insane and out of touch. That was until I listened to what they had to say. While I won't go as far as to say I had an epiphany and am now a born again believer, their demands no longer seem so ridiculous.

Play.tm recently interviewed one of the people at the forefront of the movement, Floridian lawyer Jack Thompson. When asked whether parents should be held responsible for censoring games from children and the easily influenced, part of his answer stated 'All I am trying to do is get the US to the UK (and elsewhere) system that stops the sale of adult games to kids'.

Their movement is striving for what the UK and Europe has.

It's a simple demand—rate games by age. That's it.

Looking at all the publicity around what Jack and the movement are trying to achieve, it's easy to believe that they are after something else, like banning violent videogames outright. Not so, says Jack. 'Any policy to stop the sale of adult games to adults? No way'.

If all he is trying to achieve is parity with other nations, is that necessarily a bad thing? The lack of violent video game related deaths and high profile lawsuits seem to show the system works and everyone copes just fine.

How the Ratings System Works in Britain

At age 16 I convinced my parents to buy me the original *Grand Theft Auto [GTA]*—even in 1998 the retailer refused to sell me the game. The fact my parents trusted me enough to play the game and not, say, steal my father's car and commit murder is a decision they took and one that a retailer can't be expected to. It's not a great leap to see this system implemented across the US and it's hard to see whom it would harm.

The videogame rating system employed in the UK has stood up to everything thrown at it and, to my knowledge, has never seen a game banned. In Australia the game *Reservoir Dogs* was pulled from the shelves. In England, you can get it in Tesco [a grocery chain]. They'll also sell you *Grand Theft Auto*. *Bully* [game]? Now discounted in most stores. Get it while it's hot.

All this in a country that hasn't seen a single organised rally to ban a game. When *Grand Theft Auto: San Andreas* was released I was near the front of the midnight queue. The gamer in front of me was lucky enough to look under 18 and was asked for ID at the counter. He showed a card, paid and collected his copy. Both he and I walked out of the shop unhindered—nobody accused us of being evil or baby killers or being responsible for the end of civilised society.

Soon after, the UK gaming industry body, ELSPA, declared *San Andreas* to be the fastest selling game since records began, shifting million copies in just nine days. The director general of ELSPA, Roger Bennett, was quoted as saying, 'What has been so satisfying is the exceptionally high level of awareness for both *GTA* and video games in general, in both media coverage and the public consciousness.' No references to regrettable outbreaks of violence, public rioting or mass protests in London.

If this model can be transplanted to continental America, it's hard to find anyone who wouldn't benefit. While the world wouldn't instantly become a better place it's fair to say that protests would end and videogame violence would no longer hit the negative press as much as it does now. If asking for ID stops one person killing another, it's surely worth doing. Artier all, as Jack said in our interview, 'if [real life violence by gamers] continues, you're going to see a call for a total *ban*.'

It's time both sides of this dispute, the angry American parents and the aloof games industry, worked together to help change the way games are sold. ID is cheap and plentiful—drivers licences and passports aren't hard to request, wherever you are.

In perhaps the best example of the flaws in the American rating system, *Grand Theft Auto: San Andreas* was pulled from Wal-mart's shelves during the 'hot coffee' scandal, where hidden sex scenes were found in the game. Yet from the start to the finish of this controversy, the game was still available on Asda's [a British store similar to Wal-Mart] shelves across the UK. The only difference is the rating system in place—Wal-mart rated the game as Mature while Asda sold it as an 18-rated game.

If all it takes to end this crisis is a set of new age rating labels, I'd like to volunteer my printer to help get the US ready for the next *Grand Theft Auto*. Alright, it's not out till November [2007], but it's only a cheap inkjet—it takes some time to warm up. Granted, printing off ten million labels on my desk-top printer is a bit of a silly thing to do, but then so are mass riots over the wrong sticker.

| "Parents and physicians should pay careful attention to the actual content of any M-rated video game that their children might play, particularly since the M-rating indicates that the intended audience is for ages seventeen years and older."

Video Game Ratings Are Often Inaccurate

Kimberly M. Thompson, Karen Tepichin, and Kevin Haninger

The following viewpoint contains the results of a study performed by associate professor Kimberly M. Thompson and researchers Karen Tepichin and Kevin Haninger for the Kids Risk Project at Harvard's School of Public Health. In the study, the authors compared descriptors assigned by the Entertainment Software Rating Board (ESRB) for games rated M (mature) with descriptors they agreed upon while playing thirty-six randomly selected M-rated games. The study concludes that the assignment of descriptors by the ESRB is inconsistent, and the authors recommend that parents be careful relying on ESRB's M-rating for their children.

Kimberly M. Thomspon, Karen Tepichin, and Kevin Haninger, "Content and Ratings of Mature-Rated Video Games," *Archives of Pediatrics and Adolescent Medicine*, vol. 160, April 2006, pp. 402–410. Copyright © 2006 American Medical Association. All rights reserved. Reproduced by permission.

As you read, consider the following questions:

1. According to the authors, what percentage of M-rated games does the Federal Trade Commission say are purchased for children younger than seventeen years?

2. How do the authors say the absence of a content descriptor should be interpreted by parents?

3. What do the authors recommend the Entertainment Software Rating Board should do?

The Entertainment Software Rating Board (ESRB) assigns age-based rating symbols and content descriptors that appear on video game boxes to inform consumers about game content. To receive a rating, game manufacturers submit videotaped footage and other information to the ESRB for review by 3 independent raters. We previously quantified the content of video games rated E (for "everyone") and T (for "teen") and observed content that could warrant ESRB content descriptors in games lacking such content descriptors. Although video games rated M (for "mature") continue to raise concerns and attract media attention, to our knowledge, no study to date quantifies the content of potential concern to physicians, parents, and others or the correspondence between game content and the ESRB content descriptors displayed on the game box.

Recent studies document the increasing popularity of video games among children and adolescents, with 91% or 8- to 18-year-olds reporting that they played a console video game at least once. In the last 5 years, the average time spent playing video games by 8- to 18-year-olds nearly doubled from 26 to 49 minutes per day. The results indicate an average of 2.1 video game consoles per home, with 31% of children and adolescents surveyed reporting 3 or more consoles. Children and adolescents with video game consoles in their rooms reported significantly more time spent playing video games, while parental rules restricting TV and video game use appear to reduce reported video game play time. Unfortunately, the same survey did not ask about M-rated video games played. However, 27% and 65% of respondents reported they had played *Duke Nukem* or *Grand Theft Auto*, respectively; 12% reported playing a game of which their parents would disapprove; and only 17% indicated that their parents check the ratings on games.

In addition, the most recent Federal Trade Commission report on marketing violent entertainment to children cited industry data showing that in 2002 consumers purchased nearly 40% of M-rated video games for children younger than 17 years. The Federal Trade Commission also reported that 69% of unaccompanied children aged 13 to 16 years participating in its mystery shopper survey successfully purchased M-rated video games. Industry data also identified M-rated *Grand Theft Auto: San Andreas* and *Halo 2* as the best-selling video games of 2004. A national study of 5,756 students in Canada found that approximately 22% of boys in grades 3 through 6 and 50% of boys in grades 7 through 10 identified 1 or more M-rated video games among their 3 favorite games. Thus, while the M-rating should theoretically lead to restrictions on children's exposure to the content in these games, the limited existing data suggest that many children younger than 17 years currently play M-rated video games.

Legislative efforts to restrict the sale of violent video games to minors and lawsuits covered in the popular media demonstrate the public concern about the potential health impacts of video games on children. With respect to video games, a meta-analysis of experimental and nonexperimental studies found that playing violent video games increased aggression in children and young adults. A recent experimental study of mostly adults, designed to detect only moderate or large effects, did not find an increase in aggressive thoughts or behaviors after 1 month of playing an M-rated online fantasy game. Given

Profanity in Video Games

These games are divided by the way their language is described in each game's rating. The uses of profanity in several of the games with no language warning meet or exceed those described as having "strong language" or "mild language."

		No. of observed uses of profanity per hour		
Game title	Total	Dialogue or writing	Song lyrics	Gestures
Strong language				
BMX XXX	201	166	35	
Cold Winter	3	3		
Fallout: Brotherhood of Steel	13	13		
Grand Theft Auto: Vice City	23	23		
Hitman: Contracts	0	0		
Run Like Hell	16	16		
Shadow Man: 2econd Coming	17	17		
Syphon Filter: The Omega Strain	3	3		
The Chronicles of Riddick: Escape from Butcher Bay	57	56		1
Mild language				
Rogue Ops	5	5		
No descriptors				
Brute Force	3	3		
Drakengard	2	2		
Eternal Darkness: Sanity's Requiem	1	1		
Gungrave	7	7		
Max Payne	9	9		
McFarlane's Evil Prophecy	3	3		
Metal Gear Solid: The Twin Snakes	1	1		
Onimusha 2: Samurai's Destiny	1	1		

[CONTINUED]

the very limited evidence, understanding the effects of video games on brain processing, learning, attitudes, and behaviors requires additional research, and currently, health care profes-

[CONTINUED]

Profanity in Video Games

These games are divided by the way their language is described in each game's rating. The uses of profanity in several of the games with no language warning meet or exceed those described as having "strong language" or "mild language."

| Game title | Total | No. of observed uses of profanity per hour | | |
		Dialogue or writing	Song lyrics	Gestures
No descriptors [continued]				
Red Faction II	9	9		
Silent Hill 2	3	3		
Silent Scope Complete	1	1		
Soldier of Fortune II: Double Helix	1	1		
The Thing	21	21		
Twisted Metal: Black	4	4		
Unreal II: The Awakening	7	7		

TAKEN FROM: Kimberly M. Thompson, Karen Tepichin, and Kevin Haninger, "Content and Ratings of Mature-Rated Video Games," *Archives of Pediatrics and Adolescent Medicine*, April 2005.

sionals must offer advice to parents in the absence of good data from rigorous longitudinal studies. To our knowledge, this study provides the first set of quantitative data available to physicians and parents to help them better understand the content of M-rated video games and the accuracy of the rating information provided.

How the Study Was Conducted

We created a database of all 147 M-rated video game titles scheduled for release on the major video game consoles (Xbox [Microsoft Corporation], GameCube [Nintendo of America], and PlayStation 2 [Sony Computer Entertainment America]) in the United States by April 1, 2004. Using data from the ESRB and several video game Web sites, we verified the release of each game title, recorded the ESRB-assigned content descriptors, and classified each game title by 1 of 10 primary genres.

We randomly selected 25% (37) of the 147 M-rated video game titles to play. However, given the postponed release of *Painkiller* until 2006, we played only 36 games. All of the games played remain available for sale or rental. When possible, we purchased or rented the games with their original game manuals intact. For consistency, a research assistant with considerable video-gaming experience played the entire random sample of video games and recorded all game play on DVD for later coding. The player first read the manual and played the game to become familiar with the game features, then restarted the video game from the beginning and recorded at least 1 hour of game play, including any required game introductions and setup. . . .

To quantify the amount of violence in each game, we divided the recorded game play into 1-second intervals and noted whether each second of game play contained acts of violence. For each second of game play not already coded as "committing violence," we coded the second as "planning violence" if it showed a character planning acts of violence, as "depicting injuries" if it depicted injuries from violence, or as "not violent" if it failed to meet either of these criteria. To further characterize the overall portrayal of violence, we used 3 categories to separately code the highest (and most severe) portrayal of injuries depicted to human and nonhuman characters using a method previously shown to provide good agreement between independent coders. We also noted the types of weapons used for violence, whether the player could select or modify these weapons, whether violence resulted in injury or death, the number of human and nonhuman deaths from violence, whether injuring or killing human and nonhuman characters was rewarded or was required to advance in the game, and whether destroying objects was rewarded or required to advance in the game, although we did not code the destruction of objects as violence. To quantify the amount of blood, we noted whether each second of game play depicted blood and further identified whether each second depicted human or nonhuman blood. We did not code blood as a depiction of injury unless the blood came from a known act of violence. We also noted whether the game depicted the mutilation or severing of body parts. To quantify the amount of sexual themes, we noted whether each second of game play depicted sexual behaviors, sexual dialogue, and/or nudity. We also noted the sex of the characters involved and whether the player could play each game as a male or female character. To quantify profanity, we counted each occurrence and noted the specific gesture or word(s) used. We noted whether the profanity occurred in the game as dialogue, written text, or song lyrics. To quantify the amount of alcohol, tobacco, and drugs in the game, we noted whether each second of game play depicted any type of substance, and we separately noted whether each second involved substance use. Finally, we counted the number of seconds of game play that depicted gambling. . . .

Results of the Study

The results of our study suggest that parents and physicians should pay careful attention to the actual content of any M-rated video game that their children might play, particularly since the M-rating indicates that the intended audience is for ages 17 years and older. Compared with our studies of T-rated video games, we found significantly more blood, severe injuries, and human deaths in M-rated games, although we also found a significantly smaller percentage of violent game play in M-rated video games. We believe that current discussions about restricting children's access to violent games may miss the reality that both T-rated and M-rated games contain significant amounts of violence.

These results confirm that the presence of an ESRB content descriptor means that game players likely will find the indicated content in the game but that parents should not interpret the absence of a content descriptor to mean the absence of content. Parents should recognize that the content descriptors on M-rated video games usually do not provide information about all types of content in the game, notably the depiction of substances. Our observation that 20 (56%) of 36 games depicted substances while only 1 game (3%) received a content descriptor for substances should motivate consideration of children's exposure to substances in video games (and more broadly in all media). While some might argue about the need to provide content descriptors for M-rated video games given the intended audience of ages 17 years and older, we note that the ESRB does not provide specific criteria for assigning content descriptors. Even within a rating category, the ESRB assigns content descriptors to some games but not others with the same content, which creates confusion for parents who seek accurate and consistent rating information. We emphasize that the ESRB should provide greater clarity about its content descriptors and rating standards. In addition, since our studies consistently found content for which the ESRB did not assign content descriptors, we continue to believe that the ESRB should play the video games before assigning its ratings and provide assurance to parents and to the public about the quality of the rating information.

This study relies on the same methods and consequently implies the same methodological limitations as our other studies of video games. In this study, our random sample represented only 25% of M-rated video games with 1 game in the sample not reaching the market prior to completion of the study. In the context of evolving games and ratings, this sample represents a cross-section of M-rated video games. We

Skokie Public Library
215 Oakton St
Skokie, IL 60077

Items that you checked out

Title:
Video games / Laurie Willis, book editor.
ID: 31232003663764
Due: Tuesday, May 02, 2017

Total items: 1
Account balance: $0.00
Tuesday, April 11, 2017 1:00 PM
Ready for pickup: 0

Renew online: www.skokielibrary.info
Renew by phone: (847) 673-2675

Thank you for using the Express Check
Out

did not unlock additional material in games by entering codes (e.g., from Web sites), but parents should know that codes can alter game play. The ESRB's recent decision to change the rating of *Grand Theft Auto: San Andreas* from M to AO (for "adults only") resulted from the ability of players to unlock sexually explicit content. Parents should look for the ESRB warning "Game Experience May Change During Online Play" and recognize that online game play may not reflect the game's original rating and content descriptors.

We emphasize that no study or rating system can replace parental engagement with children and adolescents experiencing video games and that more research is needed to understand the health impacts of video games on children and adolescents.

Parents and physicians should recognize that popular M-rated video games contain a wide range of content and may expose children and adolescents to messages that may negatively influence their perceptions, attitudes, and behaviors.

> "Self-regulation is the only acceptable
> solution to concerns about children
> playing violent video games."

Video Games Should Not Be Regulated by Legislation

Gregory Kenyota

In the following viewpoint, Gregory Kenyota contends that legislators are wasting time and taxpayer money proposing unconstitutional legislation that would regulate video games. He believes that games are protected by the First Amendment (freedom of speech). Instead, he states that the Entertainment Software Rating Board (ESRB) should continue to improve the ratings system and parents should be educated to make good use of the system. Kenyota is a student at Fordham University School of Law.

As you read, consider the following questions:

1. Why does the author believe that video games should not be blamed for the Virginia Tech shootings?

2. According to this viewpoint, what has the Federal Trade Commission said about the Entertainment Software Rating Board?

Gregory Kenyota, "Thinking of the Children: The Failure of Violent Video Game Laws (Conclusion)," *Fordham Intellectual Property, Media & Entertainment Law Journal*, Spring 2008, pp. 812–815. Copyright © 2008 Fordham University, School of Law. Reproduced by permission of the publisher and the author.

3. What does the author say is the proper solution for legislators?

On April 16, 2007, a lone gunman went on a shooting spree on the Virginia Tech campus, killing thirty people. Later that night, Dr. Phil McGraw, the host of the *Dr. Phil* show, went on *Larry King Live* to discuss the Virginia Tech shooting and stated that:

> [T]he problem is we are programming these people as a society. You cannot tell me—common sense tells you that if these kids are playing video games, where they're on a mass killing spree in a video game, it's glamorized on the big screen, it's become part of the fiber of our society. You take that and mix it with a psychopath, a sociopath or someone suffering from mental illness and add in a dose of rage, the suggestibility is too high. And we're going to have to start dealing with that. We're going to have to start addressing those issues and recognizing that the mass murders [sic] of tomorrow are the children of today that are being programmed with this massive violence overdose.

The call to blame video games was reminiscent of the Columbine [High School] shootings eight years earlier. Unlike Columbine, where the shooters had some connections to video games, subsequent investigations of the Virginia Tech shooter by police found "[n]ot a single video game, console or gaming gadget" and the shooter's suite-mate "said he had never seen [the shooter] play video games." Despite this lack of evidence, some people like attorney Jack Thompson still blame video games for the Virginia Tech shooting.

The recent controversies and legislation over violent video games are clear examples of critics blaming violent video games for negative effects without any support for those accusations. Video games did not turn the Virginia Tech shooter into a killer. The research on violent video games has not found any causal connection between violent video games and

Video Games Are Not to Blame for School Shootings

As the leader of an organization that represents video game creators from all over the world, [Jason] Della Rocca knows the routine all too well.

Someone opens fire on a school campus. Someone blames video games. His phone starts ringing. People start asking him questions like, "So how bad are these games anyway?"

Of course, he also knows that this is far from the first time in history that a young form of pop culture has been blamed for any number of society's ills. Rock and roll was the bad guy in the 1950s. Jazz was the bad guy in the 1930s. . . .

For those who didn't grow up playing video games, the appeal of a game like *Counter-Strike* can be hard to comprehend. It can be difficult to understand that the game promotes communication and team work. It can be hard to fathom how players who love to run around gunning down their virtual enemies do not have even the slightest desire to shoot a person in real life.

Winda Benedetti,
"Were Video Games to Blame for Massacre?"
April 20, 2007. www.msnbc.msn.com.

children committing violent acts. The need to regulate violent video games because of the harm they supposedly cause is illusory at best.

Legislators Need to Stop Proposing Unconstitutional Legislation

Legislators therefore need to stop attempting to regulate violent video games with laws that courts have repeatedly held are unconstitutional. The First Amendment protects the content of violent video games and any law attempting to regulate them based on their violent content will be subject to a strict scrutiny analysis. The exceptions to the First Amendment proffered by the states that video games should fall under such as obscenity, content harmful to minors, and incitement do not apply to violent video games. There is no need for these laws and passing them only ends up costing taxpayers money after the courts invalidate them. District Judge Brady of the Middle District Court of Louisiana admonished the Louisiana legislature for its violent video game legislation in stating:

> This Court is dumbfounded that the Attorney General and the State are in the position of having to pay taxpayer money as attorney's fees and costs in this lawsuit. The Act which this Court found unconstitutional passed through committees in both the State House and Senate, then through the full House and Senate, and to be promptly signed by the Governor. There are lawyers at each stage of this process. Some of the members of these committees are themselves lawyers. Presumably, they have staff members who are attorneys as well. The State House and Senate certainly have staff members who are attorneys. The governor has additional attorneys—the executive counsel. Prior to the passage of the Act, there were a number of reported cases from a number of jurisdictions which held similar statutes to be unconstitutional (and in which the defendant was ordered to pay substantial attorney's fees). The Court wonders why nobody objected to the enactment of this statute. In this court's view, the taxpayers deserve more from their elected officials.

Self-Regulation Is the Best Solution

Self-regulation is the only acceptable solution to concerns about children playing violent video games. The Federal government in 1994 wanted the game industry to self-regulate and that is exactly what the video game industry has been doing with the ESRB [Entertainment Software Rating Board]. The FTC [Federal Trade Commission] has consistently found that the ESRB has improved its ratings system and awareness ever since it first started investigating it. If a video game developer develops a game that the ESRB considers too violent, the video game retailers and the video game manufacturers will also take actions that will make sure the game does not even make it to publication. There is no evidence that the ESRB has failed as a ratings system in such a way that the government needs to step in and take over.

The proper solution for legislators is to work with the video game industry, not against them. ESA [Entertainment Software Association] senior VP [Vice President], and general counsel Gail Markels has stated that "[i]t couldn't be clearer that the real answer is not regulation, but education of parents to empower them to use the video game rating system, parental controls in game consoles, and other available tools. . . We look forward to working with any elected official to help educate parents about making appropriate video game choices for their unique families." Maybe someday legislators across the country will spend their time and taxpayers' money on educating parents rather than trying to regulate the video game industry.

Periodical Bibliography

The following articles have been selected to supplement the diverse views presented in this chapter.

Jerry Bonner | "How to Fix the Ratings System," *Electronic Gaming Monthly*, April 2008.

Patrick R. Byrd | "It's All Fun and Games Until Someone Gets Hurt: The Effectiveness of Proposed Video-Game Legislation on Reducing Violence in Children," *Houston Law Review*, April 26, 2007.

N'Gai Croal | "The Game-Ratings Game," *Newsweek*, April 21, 2008.

Anton Galang | "The Watchful Eye of Gaming," *PC Magazine*, September 4, 2007.

Kevin Haninger and Kimberly M. Thompson | "Content and Ratings of Teen-Rated Video Games," *JAMA*, February 18, 2004.

Mary Jane Irwin | "Rated V for Violence," *PC Magazine*, March 7, 2006.

Patrick Joynt | "Games vs. Politics," *PC Magazine*, August 22, 2006.

Daniel Koffler | "Grand Theft Scapegoat: The Ridiculous Jihad Against Video Games," *Reason*, October 2005.

Joelle Tessler | "Video Game Ratings: A Hot-Button Issue," *CQ Weekly*, August 14, 2006, p. 2220–21.

Jason Tocci | "Seeking Truth in Video Game Ratings," *International Journal of Communication*, 2008.

Barbara Dafoe Whitehead | "Parents Need Help: Restricting Access to Video Games," *Commonweal*, January 28, 2005.

For Further Discussion

Chapter 1

1. Marc Prensky asserts that playing video games helps children learn. Philip A. Chan and Terry Rabinowitz blame video games for poor grades. Do you agree completely with either argument? Is it possible that each is partially right? Use examples from the viewpoints to support your answer.

2. Olivia and Kurt Bruner argue that gaming is a waste of time. Jennifer Seter Wagner takes this idea one step further and talks about playing video games as an addiction. Steven Johnson claims that video games are no more addictive than other pleasurable activities. According to Henry Jenkins, video games don't waste time but help children to learn time management skills. What do you think about time spent playing video games? Is it time wasted? Is it possible to be addicted to video games? Is everyone who plays video games addicted? Use arguments from the viewpoints to support your answers.

3. The surveys described by Martin J. Atherton and James A. Metcalf conclude that playing video games contributes to obesity in children. Elisabeth Hayes and Lauren Silberman assert that gaming can improve motivation and performance in sports. How do you believe playing video games relates to obesity and physical activity? Is this changing as newer games are released?

Chapter 2

1. David Leonard argues that video games promote racial stereotypes. Elizabeth Sweedyk and Marianne de Laet discuss sexual stereotyping in games. On the other hand,

Gonzalo Frasca discusses video games that teach social tolerance, and John C. Beck and Mitchell Wade assert that games transcend gender roles. Do you believe stereotyping in video games is a problem? Explain why or why not, using examples cited in the viewpoints.

2. Jenny McCartney asserts that some video games are immoral and should not be played by anyone. James Paul Gee claims that video games can be good for the soul. What characteristics of video games do you see as contributing negatively to society's morality? What characteristics contribute positively, either to society or to individual well-being?

Chapter 3

1. Craig A. Anderson claims that playing violent video games causes aggressive behavior. David Kushner contends that there is no causal link between violent games and aggression. What evidence does each author offer to support his argument? Which argument seems stronger? Why?

2. Dan Costa argues that video games should not be used to teach war. Grace Jean discusses *America's Army* as a good training tool for the military. Do you see advantages to video games that can be used for military training? Do you see disadvantages? Use examples from the viewpoints to support your answers.

3. Charles Herold contends that playing violent video games actually reduces violence in the real world. Christopher J. Ferguson argues that people should be held responsible for violent acts they commit, and games and other media should not be used as scapegoats. Compare their arguments to those of Craig A. Anderson and David Kushner. Considering all of these viewpoints, what do you believe is the relationship between video games and violence in the real world? What arguments from the viewpoints support your answer?

Chapter 4

1. Hillary Rodham Clinton believes that video games should be regulated by legislation. James Paterson contends that parents and the gaming industry should work together to regulate game use. After considering the arguments in each of these viewpoints, who do you believe should control what video games children play—the law, the gaming industry, parents, or a combination of these? Why?

2. Kimberly M. Thomspon, Karen Tepichin, and Kevin Haninger point out games that they believe are inaccurately rated by the Entertainment Software Rating Board (ESRB). Gregory Kenyota contends that legislation governing video gaming is unconstitutional and that the ESRB should continue to be responsible for rating video games. Do you believe that the ESRB ratings are accurate? Are they effective? Refer to any of the viewpoints in this chapter to support your answer.

Organizations to Contact

The editors have compiled the following list of organizations concerned with the issues debated in this book. The descriptions are derived from materials provided by the organizations. All have publications or information available for interested readers. The list was compiled on the date of publication of the present volume; the information provided here may change. Be aware that many organizations take several weeks or longer to respond to inquiries, so allow as much time as possible.

Center for Media Literacy (CML)
23852 Pacific Coast Highway, #472, Malibu, CA   90265
(310) 456-1225 • fax: (310) 456-0020
e-mail: cml@medialit.org
Web site: www.medialit.org

The Center for Media Literacy (CML) works to help citizens, especially the young, develop critical thinking and media production skills needed to make wise choices in their use of media. CML's Web site includes information and lesson plans for parents and teachers and a downloadable document, *Literacy for the 21st Century: An Overview & Orientation Guide to Media Literacy Education.*

Center for Successful Parenting
e-mail: csp@onrampamerica.net
Web site: www.sosparents.org

The Center for Successful Parenting believes that violent video games have a negative impact on child development. The organization stresses grassroots activism to eliminate the marketing of violent media to children. The center's Web site offers information on game ratings and a few studies showing the detrimental effect violent video games have on brain development.

Center on Media and Child Health (CMCH)
300 Longwood Avenue, Boston, MA   02115
(617) 355-2000
e-mail: cmch@childrens.harvard.edu
Web site: www.cmch.tv

The Center on Media and Child Health (CMCH) is a collaboration between Childrens' Hospital Boston, Harvard Medical School, and Harvard School of Public Health. CMCH performs research that seeks to educate and empower children and those who care for them, so that they can create and consume media in ways that optimize health and development. The organization's Web site includes tips and guidance for parents and teachers on using video games safely. CMCH publishes an online e-newsletter and a blog.

Common Sense Media
650 Townsend Street, Suite 375, San Francisco, CA   94103
(415) 863-0600
Web site: www.commonsensemedia.org

Common Sense Media is an organization devoted to improving the media experiences of children and families. It advocates media literacy rather than censorship to help children and parents navigate the barrage of media influences that impact people daily. The organization offers reviews of video games and other media products on its Web site.

Entertainment Consumers Association (ECA)
64 Danbury Road, Suite 700, Wilton, CT   06897-4406
(203) 761-6180 • fax: (203) 761-6184
e-mail: feedback@theeca.com
Web site: www.theeca.com

The Entertainment Consumers Association (ECA) is a nonprofit organization designed to serve the needs of video game players through advocacy, consumer rights initiatives, and political lobbying. The ECA Web site includes position papers on violence in video games, video game regulations, and safe play in online games. ECA also distributes an online newsletter regarding the industry and consumer events.

Entertainment Merchants Association (EMA)

16530 Ventura Boulevard, Suite 400, Encino, CA   91436
(818) 385-1500 • fax: (818) 385-0567
Web site: www.entmerch.org

The Entertainment Merchants Association (EMA) is a nonprofit international trade association designed to promote, protect, and provide a forum for the common business interests of those engaged in the sale, rental, and licensed reproduction of entertainment software such as DVDs and video games. The EMA's Web site includes information on video game ratings.

Entertainment Software Association (ESA)

575 Seventh Street NW, Suite 300, Washington, DC   20004
e-mail: esa@theesa.com
Web site: www.theesa.com

The Entertainment Software Association (ESA) is an American association exclusively dedicated to serving the business and public affairs needs of video game companies. The ESA Web site offers sections on facts and statistics, public policy and legal issues, games in daily life, game news, and resources for parents.

Entertainment Software Rating Board (ESRB)

317 Madison Avenue, 22nd Floor, New York, NY   10017
Web site: www.esrb.org

Established in 1994, the Entertainment Software Rating Board (ESRB) is a nonprofit regulatory board created by the Entertainment Software Association. The board rates video games based on content and the targeted age group. Game-specific ratings are available on the Web site. The ESRB publishes a bimonthly online newsletter for parents called *ParenTools*. The

Web site also contains information pages on recent industry news, parent and consumer protection, and education and outreach programs.

International Game Developers Association (IGDA)
19 Mantua Road, Mt. Royal, NJ   08061
(856) 423-2990 • fax: (856) 423-3420
e-mail: contact@igda.org
Web site: www.igda.org

The International Game Developers Association (IGDA) is an industry association that promotes career development and fosters community interests within the field of video game design. Part of the IGDA mission is to fight censorship of video games. The IGDA Web site includes position papers on concerns over video game rating and censorship. It also publishes various papers and articles and the *IGDA Newsletter.*

Mothers Against Videogame Addiction
and Violence (MAVAV)
Web site: www.mavav.org

Mothers Against Videogame Addiction and Violence (MAVAV) believes that video game addiction is a serious epidemic and that the video game industry promotes hatred, racism, and sexism. MAVAV is dedicated to educating parents about these issues. The organization's Web site presents news, articles, and resources on video game addiction and violence.

Media Awareness Network (MNet)
1500 Merivale Road, 3rd Floor, Ottawa, Ontario   K2E 6Z5
  Canada
(613) 224 7721 • fax: (613) 224-1958
e-mail: info@media-awareness.ca
Web site: www.media-awareness.ca

Media Awareness Network (MNet) is a Canadian organization that provides educational materials and resource documents related to media and information literacy for young people.

Articles on the Media Awareness Network Web site cover news, current issues, and research on topics such as violence and stereotyping in media. The site also includes several educational games for young people.

National Institute on Media and the Family
606 Twenty-Fourth Avenue S, Suite 606
Minneapolis, MN 55454
(888) 672-5437 • fax: (612) 672-4113
Web site: www.mediafamily.org

The National Institute on Media and the Family is a nonprofit, nonpartisan organization that provides research, education, and information concerning the impact of media on children and families. The goal of the organization is to empower parents and other consumers to make informed choices about media products that will likely impact children. The institute's Web site provides reviews of video games and information on how media relates to school success, health and safety, violence and disrespect, and addiction.

On-Line Gamers Anonymous (OLGA)
PO Box 3433, Brentwood, TN 37024
(612) 245-1115
Web site: www.olganon.org

On-Line Gamers Anonymous (OLGA) is a fellowship of people sharing their experiences, strengths, and hopes to help each other recover and heal from the problems caused by excessive game playing, using a twelve-step program of recovery. OLGA/OLG-Anon provides a resource for open discussion, support, education and referrals through online chat, meetings, and discussion forums for gamers and their families.

Serious Games Initiative
1300 Pennsylvania Avenue NW, Washington, DC 20004
(207) 773-3700
e-mail: bsawyer@seriousgames.org
Web site: www.seriousgames.org

The Serious Games Initiative was founded at the Woodrow Wilson Center for International Scholars in Washington, D.C. The organization promotes the adoption of computer games for a variety of challenges facing the world today. Its main projects are Games for Health and Games for Change. The Web site includes information on both of these topics as well as an annotated list of games they consider to be examples that engage contemporary social issues in meaningful ways to foster a more just, equitable, and tolerant society.

Bibliography of Books

Richard Abanes   *What Every Parent Needs to Know About Video Games.* Eugene, OR: Harvest House Publishers, 2006.

Craig A. Anderson, Douglas A. Gentile, and Katherine E. Buckley   *Violent Video Game Effects on Children and Adolescents: Theory, Research, and Public Policy.* New York: Oxford University Press, 2007.

Brenda Brathwaite   *Sex in Video Games.* Boston, MA: Charles River Media, 2007.

David Buckingham and Rebekah Willett   *Digital Generations: Children, Young People, and New Media.* Mahwah, NJ: Lawrence Erlbaum Associates, Publishers, 2006.

Derek A. Burrill   *Die Tryin': Videogames, Masculinity, Culture.* New York: Peter Lang, 2008.

Justine Cassell and Henry Jenkins, eds.   *From Barbie to Mortal Kombat: Gender and Computer Games.* Cambridge, MA: MIT Press, 1999.

Rusel DeMaria   *Reset: Changing the Way We Look at Video Games.* San Francisco, CA: Berrett-Koehler, 2007.

David Edery and Ethan Mollick   *Changing the Game: How Video Games Are Transforming the Future of Business.* Upper Saddle River, NJ: FT Press, 2008.

James Paul Gee   *What Video Games Have to Teach Us About Learning and Literacy.* New York: Palgrave Macmillan, 2004.

Dave Grossman   *Stop Teaching Our Kids to Kill: A Call to Action Against TV, Movie and Video Game Violence.* New York: Crown, 1999.

Sarah L. Holloway   *Cyberkids: Children in the Information Age.* London: Routledge Falmer, 2003.

David Hutchison   *Playing to Learn: Video Games in the Classroom.* Westport, CT: Libraries Unlimited, 2007.

Yasmin B. Kafai   *Beyond Barbie and Mortal Kombat:*
et al, eds.   *New Perspectives on Gender and Gaming.* Cambridge, MA: MIT Press, 2008.

Brad King   *Dungeons and Dreamers: The Rise of Computer Game Culture from Geek to Chic.* New York: McGraw-Hill/Osborne, 2003.

Joseph A.   *School Shootings: What Every Parent*
Lieberman   *and Educator Needs to Know to Protect Our Children.* New York: Citadel Press, 2006.

Ken S. McAllister   *Game Work: Language, Power, and Computer Game Culture.* Tuscaloosa, AL: University of Alabama Press, 2004.

Rebecca Mileham *Powering Up: Are Computer Games Changing Our Lives?* West Sussex, England: John Wiley & Sons, 2008.

David Nichols *Brands & Gaming: The Computer*
et al *Gaming Phenomenon and Its Impact on Brands and Businesses.* Basingstoke, England: Palgrave Macmillan, 2006.

Jim Rossignol *This Gaming Life: Travels in Three Cities.* Ann Arbor, MI: University of Michigan Press, 2008.

David Williamson *How Computer Games Help Children*
Shaffer *Learn.* New York: Palgrave Macmillan, 2008.

Iain Simons and *Difficult Questions About Video*
James Newman *Games.* Nottingham, UK: Suppose Partners, 2004.

Melanie Swalwell *The Pleasures of Computer Gaming:*
and Jason Wilson, *Essays on Cultural History, Theory*
eds. *and Aesthetics.* Jefferson, NC: McFarland & Co, 2008.

T.L. Taylor *Play Between Worlds: Exploring Online Game Culture.* Cambridge, MA: MIT Press, 2006.

Valerie *Children, Gender, Video Games:*
Walkerdine *Towards a Relational Approach to Multimedia.* Basingstoke, England: Palgrave Macmillan, 2007.

| Noah Wardrip-Fruin and Pat Harrigan, eds. | *First Person: New Media as Story, Performance, and Game.* Cambridge, MA: MIT Press, 2004. |
| J. Patrick Williams | *The Players' Realm: Studies on the Culture of Video Games and Gaming.* Jefferson, NC: McFarland & Company, 2007. |

Index

Z